Mark McKnight was born in Lis........ He is an author, a teacher, a musician, a film maker and a missionary in that order. Hopefully, this arrangement will change in the not too distant future. He currently lives in Northallerton, North Yorkshire (England) but in his own words, "It's not Ireland and it's not Africa!" He has also told and written a plethora of short and longer stories. Published collections include *Msimulizi: Stories for Mwangaza, Msimulizi 2: The Green Dragon* and another as yet untitled work, no doubt beginning with the words, '*Msimulizi 3...*'

On The Road is his fourth printed work.

Adam Ansel hails from Cumberland, Maryland. He is a college dropout, a reformed hippy and part of the now infamous 'Summer Fun Experience.' Home is still in Cumberland although he visits there so infrequently as to make it a mere stopping point for his travels elsewhere. He is currently on tour with the third Mwangaza Children's Choir (and may even have sold you this book). He has directed two feature length movies (*Adventures In The Land Of Heeble, The Search For Black Mamba*) and has told and written a variety of short stories. His first published collection was *My Side Of The Rio Grande or Just Off The Kartnerstrasse*. Hopefully, (if he can find some time on tour to finish it) Adventures in the Land of Heeble will make it to the shelves this year.

On The Road is his second printed work.

Forthcoming and already available titles
by Mark McKnight

Msimulizi: Stories For Mwangaza
Msimulizi 2: The Green Dragon

500: A Collection Of Stories

The Village At The End Of The World

On The Road

By Adam Ansel

My Side Of The Rio Grande or Just Off The Kartnerstasse

Adventures In The Land Of Heeble

ON THE ROAD

BY MARK MCKNIGHT AND ADAM ANSEL

Acknowledgements

My most heartfelt gratitude is for Almighty God for pulling me out of that car wreck. Thank God 'On A Stormy Tuesday Afternoon' is just a story.

Then in no particular order, thanks are also due to Adam Ansel, my two families, the village and particularly the children of Gaba for their continuing inspiration, Pastor Peter, the Teiras, the Klemckes, the Gerlachs, the Freemans, all of the Mwangaza host familes, Baz & Vix, Mark & Andrea Rhodes and everyone who has been an encouragement, an inspiration or a muse for my creativity.
I thank you.

Copyright © 2005 by Mark McKnight

First published in 2006 by Baby Mosquito Books

The right of Mark McKnight and Adam Ansel to be identified as the authors of the Work has been asserted by them in accordance with the
Copyright, Designs and Patents Act 1988 (UK).

All applicable rights to the full extent of copyright law are reserved in any other territory where this book is distributed including but not limited to
U.S.A., Europe and Australia

All rights reserved. No part of this publication may be reproduced, stored in a retrieval system, or transmitted, in any form or by any means without the prior written permission of the publisher, nor be otherwise circulated in any form of binding or cover other than that in which it is published and without a similar condition being imposed on the subsequent purchaser.

ISBN 1-905691-00-9
ISBN 978-1-905691-00-5

This book has been typeset in Times New Roman, Bermuda Solid, Untitled, Celtic Eels, Celtic Garamond the 2nd & Walt Disney Script v4.1
All maps supplied by worldatlas.com
Printed and bound in the UK and United States by
Lightning Source Inc, LaVergne TN

Africa Renewal Ministries (USA)
P.O. Box 781671
San Antonio, TX, 78278

Tel: (210) 979-7441

http://www.africarenewal.org
info@africarenewal.org

For Pete
*You are the incarcerated visionary
Time and again we have been humbled your courage
Your unshakeable faith and unquestioning allegiance to the Father
A mere two Winter's have you sojourned in a strange house:
Yet the Lord will repay the years that the locusts have devoured*

And for
*Angella N, Angella M, Dorothy A, Dorothy N
Priscilla, Gladys, Omega, Joy, Cissy, Daphine
Leah, Jackie, Jesca, Dwayne, Freedom, Martin
Nicolas, Ponsiano, William, Malach,
Marci, Tana, Corey, Kara
James, Lillian, Sarah, Joshua
Adam and Joe David*

May the road rise to meet you,
May the wind be always at your back.
May the sun shine upon your face,
The rains fall soft upon your fields.
And, until we meet again, may God hold you in the palm of his hand.

          An Irish Blessing

CONTENTS

About The Author..11
Preface...13
Pastor Peter Speaks...15
To Fill In The Gaps...25
Ugandan Preparations...31
Visas...35
Arriving In America..41
Finally I Arrive...47
The Kids...53
Concert Day..59
School Days..69
Host Families..71
Texas..79
California..83
On The Bus...89
G.M.A. Dove Awards...93
Ministry..101
Fundraising...103
We Also Have Fun Days!...105
Back Home In Africa...111
Report On Bethany Village..117
Conclusion..121
More Information: How Can I Get Involved?.................123

On The Road
Mark McKnight & Adam Ansel

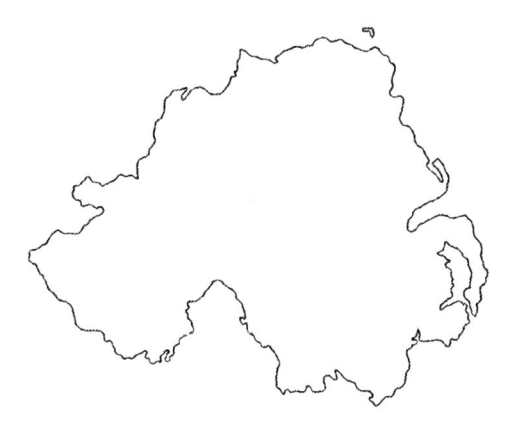

About The Author

I can tell you who the least important person in this story is. There's this wee man from just outside Belfast in Northern Ireland. He's a mediocre sound engineer but he really loves to play the saxophone. God has been working on him for a good twelve and a half years now but he doesn't seem to be making much progress. He can be hard to work with at times and he's rude too. He has a bit of experience touring so I suppose he will be good to have along – he should know what's going on!

OK, you're right – it's me. Let me get the short biography out of the way so that I can clutter the rest of the book with amusing anecdotes about tour rather than mundane details of my background.

I was born in a town called Lisburn in Northern Ireland. I grew up during a civil war of sorts but I'm from farming stock so I spent most of my childhood in the countryside gloriously untroubled by 'The Troubles.' I gave my life to the Lord on 14th November, 1992 at about 2:00am. It was at a youth weekend. At school, I was good at music so that's what I studied at college. Back in the day I was a classical flute player but someone once offered me work on the saxophone and the money was too good to turn down so I got a saxophone and learned how to play. That changed my life – suddenly I was playing in all kinds of bands. White Saturday was my first band. Our first gig we were kicked off the stage by the MC. Our second gig, nobody turned up. White Saturday broke up when I had to break up a fight between the bassist and the guitarist during a practice one rainy Friday night. Our two piece, 'P-Jazz' had much more success and even gained a certain notoriety. Unfortunately, this was not for the right reasons.

When I was twenty, God sent me to New Orleans. I was meant to be studying business but I spent most of my time playing gospel music and jazz. So when I came back to Belfast, I started my own gospel choir. Just before I graduated, someone phoned me and offered me a job teaching the African Children's Choir™ how to sing. They do some great work and I still have strong links with their organisation. I sponsor Lydia Wanjiru, one of the little girls I used to travel with. She's so cute – she keeps writing me letters asking when I'm coming back to visit. It is letters like those that keep me going.

One March afternoon back in 2002, I met Adam and Craig which was the start of a slippery downhill slope that ended with the wee man from Belfast going on tour with Mwangaza and has been the source of a great deal of worry for my parents, Adam's parents, Craig's parents and Pete's parents. I can't tell you much about Pete but please pray for him – he's going through the fire and it isn't going to end any time soon. Some day, Pete – God's just not ready for you to go yet.

When I finished my contract with the African Children's Choir, God sent me to Belfast Bible College. As part of my course, I had to do what they called a field term. I could choose to either stay in Northern Ireland or go somewhere much more interesting like Uganda. It seemed like a fairly easy choice to me so I spent 7 ½ weeks in Gaba working with James and Lillian with the Children of the Light Choir. And that was it – God had me right where he needed me.

So despite the devil's best attempts to preoccupy me, that is how I found myself on tour with Mwangaza.

Preface

It must be about a two years ago now that we were praying for my visa so that I could go on tour with Mwangaza. I had already been turned down twice by the American Embassy and things were not looking good. In one of my rare moments of brief clarity, God told that he would give me the visa if I wanted it. In fairness, he also said that this tour would be one of the most difficult things I had ever undertaken. He was right.

But this isn't the story of my own petty troubles. The story of the first Mwangaza Children's Choir was and is a journey that spans thousands of miles across Africa and the United States. It is a story of mediocre triumphs, baby steps forwards, giant steps backwards, poorly conceived practical jokes and failed romances. A story of bad attitudes, flawed personalities, poor choices, incapable employees, ugly mistakes (that may be criminally prosecutable) and potentially life threatening moments of idiocy. I speak of my own contribution to life on the road.

More importantly, it is the story of how God used and continues to use broken people like me and everyone else who was on our team to glorify His name. On The Road is the story of the grace and mercy of God. Yes, there were bad times. Yes, there were times when I thought about quitting. But God is good. <u>All</u> the time.

The only thing I can tell you is my own story. I pray that I can give you an insight into our lives and why we do what we do, even after all we have passed through. Keep the children and us in your prayers. God isn't finished with us yet.

On The Road
Mark McKnight & Adam Ansel

Chapter 1

PASTOR PETER SPEAKS

Pastor Peter Kasirivu is the head pastor of Gaba Community Church and came to Gaba for the first time on Christmas day, 1987. He's also one of the main reasons I would rather work for this organization than any other. Here is what Peter says in his own words.

"My pastor told me about this place that needs people to preach. So I came, I think Christmas Day, to speak to these people. And I found about probably ten or twelve people and when I came, they said please preach to us. And [when] I went back I just forgot all about it. After some time they said why don't you come and speak to us again. So I came again and I didn't really make any kind of commitment – I didn't have any desires to come here but I saw a need for a church to be established here but sincerely speaking I wasn't so much interested.

At that time I was working in the outreach department of the church. I was the coordinator of…we called it Gospel Mission Outreach. And so we used to go around the country speaking, helping, church planting so it was part of the gospel mission around the country. We used to do church planting and other things. I was working with Pastor Leo. He's now in Rwanda. He's the founder of a church called Restoration Church in Kigali. They have a church there. So he was an evangelist. So we used to work together. We would go places, speak and then hold crusades and do church planting. I wasn't really an evangelist but I was a coordinator for an evangelist. At the same time I was doing itinerant ministry. Doing conferences and things like that so we were doing both evangelism and conferences all over the country. And we had lots of success we had several churches planted. One year we planted eight churches. It was a very interesting time. And I kept on coming [to Gaba] whenever I had the time to.

I remember in around 1988 I just felt that God was speaking to me to do something but I didn't know what it was. To change the way I was working and at that time the church where I belonged had a crisis: there was a split and that split was very painful to us because half of the people left. At that time I just felt that I was at a crossroads. I needed to find out what God was telling me. Should I continue join those guys or should I come [to Gaba? Or should I do whatever I was doing?

So I went and spent a month waiting on God. Waiting to find out his will for my life. And that's when God spoke to my heart to come over here. And I really struggle with God because personally I didn't want to come. First, this was a very, very poor place. It's still very poor but it was a lot poorer. The other thing, it was so backward, I didn't see that a man can make a future here. So that was a big challenge to me too. So I came and said Lord I've come. When I said yes, I remember that God gave me peace but not only that he opened my eyes to the realities and the potential that lay in this place. I came back from where I was and told my pastor that God has spoken to me to go to Gaba. My pastor was a very spiritual man. He's gone to be with the Lord now. He said, "If God has told you go for it."

So when I said yes to God and came, I told the few people who were here, there were around fifteen, I told them God has spoken to me to come. And they were so happy but also God opened my eyes to the realities of what was happening here because for the first time I realized that this place was very beautiful. [The author agrees] And then secondly I realized that this is virgin soil: you can do anything you want here in terms of ministry. So I started getting very excited about what God can do here. So that became a very interesting experience for me of saying yes because I started dreaming bigger dreams in life. Originally I was thinking of going for a masters program but then I felt God wants me to be here now and to stay.

So in staying, several things happened. We had a very simple structure [for a church building]. It was probably...it was slightly over 20 feet by 12. Probably 30 feet by 12. It was a tiny thing here. And that's where we started and it had papyrus on top and that was the church structure. And we had 15 members – people who were coming to church. And the challenge was how do you get from this backward situation, from a place which doesn't have any hope, a place, a people who cannot even pay your salary or pay for your house to where we are now? So that was the big challenge.

One challenge was there was a lot of witchcraft here. Where we are standing just in front of us, just in front of the church there was a shrine. You know, the people here have superstition that the gods (the gods with a small g) work better on the shores of the lake. So because of that, all the way from I don't know how many hundreds of years, there is more worship of evil spirits on the shores of the lake. And there are lots of superstitions about the god of the lake and the gods of the water and things like that. So this whole place was full of shrines. There were at least twenty shrines in this area. So there was so much witchcraft and when you start looking at, when you go into spiritual warfare you realize that when there's so much witchcraft, there's more resistance to the gospel. And even when you preach you don't have much freedom in speaking because there's a spiritual resistance, a demonic type of influence. So that's the feeling you would get when you came here. That's the feeling I would get.

The other problem was poverty. This place was so poor that most of the houses in this village were papyrus roofed – they didn't have any roofing sheets on. So what you see today, I mean, it was... this was a bad place. Now the road coming to Gaba, it was one of the worst roads that I remember, because just to get from town to here, it would take you an hour. And there were so many potholes in the road that the only taxis that were coming to the village were Landrovers; you know these heavy land rovers which would maneuver the potholes. So it was tough. And of course the people here were a mix of fishermen and small traders. We still have fishermen but that was mostly the trade. So it was kind of a simple lifestyle and the people were simple people who needed lots of help. That's the kind of environment that we came.

When I came in, I start riding my bicycle from town to here and back. And it was so hard because sometimes you would have a Wednesday service and a bible study and only one person who comes for bible study. When you've ridden a bicycle for 12 miles to come and 12 miles back and there is only one person, it is challenging. So later on I had to move and stay in the village. I rented a room, a tiny room, and I started of with a few ladies and a few men who were with us here when we started. And God started moving for sure.

Now what I haven't told you is that earlier on there was an attempt to plant a church. But that attempt failed because they had gathered as a church but then there was a fight with the people who had started it and there was a split. So when we came in, there was almost no church because there had been wars between them. Now looking back, I know that that was spiritual warfare. The enemy didn't want a church here. There were several other churches who tried to plant in this community and they failed. So it was mainly spiritual warfare. That's what I can really say. So when I came in, I realized that it takes more than the preaching and evangelism to get this thing going because we tried. We knocked on people's doors and did personal evangelism. We did open air rallies. We did everything that you can think about. But I want to tell you that we miserably failed. I mean, you could get ten people coming, saying yes to Jesus and end up having none of those in church. I remember one time we did a rally for a week and we had 40 people who said yes to Jesus. And at the end of the rally, we had a full house. From 15 or 20 to 60. But two weeks later we were back to our original number. And we had done everything. I had done follow up: we had done everything that we could do to help people to stay. So we realized that there's a spiritual problem which I hadn't realized before. So, the Lord started showing us that there is more witchcraft here than we thought.

We had also political resistance – they said you can't pray at night. We had started in the evening. They resisted us. They actually beat up two of my...no four of my people who were here, praying in the night in the tent. So we had those challenges.

So that's when God started showing us that it's time to pray. I remember we would come in the night and just...sometimes I would be alone here just praying at nights. Just spending time talking to God and praying. Nights praying. Praying and praying and praying. And the more we began praying, the more we started feeling the freedom. You know the spiritual freedom. Later on other people joined me and we prayed and we fasted and we spent time in the presence of God. And the more we prayed, the more we started seeing God working. I remember something very interesting. Once, we were in here for a bible study on a Wednesday night and we heard people shouting in the community. We didn't know what was happening. Only to find out when we went out that the shrine next door had caught fire. And of course for them they thought it was an accident but for me that was an answer to prayer. And that encouraged us that we needed to pray more. The witch doctor was a bit nasty. He would try to torment us in a way. Just to try to show us that we are nothing and nobody. But you know what? God had the victory. I remember one time he used to tie his sheep in our compound. And you know, sheep were brought here, the sheep were brought as a sacrifice by the people who had come to consult the evil spirit. So one time he tied one of his sheep in our compound and the thing just died in the compound.

From that day he feared the Christians. He never brought any of his animals in our compound.

The major thing that really gave us a breakthrough was the government itself, because they bought a big chunk of land here. They cleared it and they decided to put a new pumping station – a water pumping station. Now what is interesting is that one time we were here and we started hearing the bulldozers and the Caterpillars and all these earth movers and what were they doing? They were clearing the land. What they did was to pay off all the guys, all the people who had small houses in the area that used to be called Kinyambuzi. Kinyambuzi means a place where they eat goats. That was a nickname for the area because there were so many shrines and the witchdoctors used to ask people to bring goats for sacrifice. So people called it the place where they eat goats. Now this was the place that was cleared to put the water pumping station. There were more than ten shrines that had to be moved so they paid these guys off and the guys had to go to another place. Most of them went to other villages so they left our area. To me that was an answer to prayer. That God fought our battles by getting the witchdoctors off our community.

Miracles like that started happening and as those things were happening, the numbers in the church increased. And as they increased, we decided to break the structure and we borrowed a tent. It was a huge tent. And that was a very, very interesting breakthrough for us. The huge tent that we put on wasn't so big but it was huge for our community. It was about 300 seater. So we pitched the tent and we started evangelizing and continued our prayer meetings. Our prayer meeting still goes on up to today. There's a prayer meeting every weekend. Every Friday. It's been going on for the last 12 years and God has kept it moving. So that was a major breakthrough with the tent coming in and people starting to come to church.

Then we started realizing a few things. One, the children were not going to school. I personally loved going to school. I loved school because that is the hope of the African child – there's not much opportunity here if you haven't gone to school. If someone has gone to school, even for a few years, it is easier to get a job. But many, many kids were not going to school and you know, here you have to pay to go to school. And the parents could not afford. So that became a burden to me. And what is interesting is that God started using things and other opportunities to help us to get help for the children.

One of them was, I'm very good at repairing electricity so a friend of mine, he was doing some work for a certain organization and they needed someone to fix their electricity. So he came to me and said would you like to help these people? I said of course. So I went and helped and they paid me some money. So whenever they had a problem they would call me and then I would go and repair for these people. I did not know that these people were a big organization. So I asked them one time, "What do you do?"

They said, "Our organization is called Compassion International and we take care of children."

I said "Oh, I'm a pastor and I'm in this village where kids are not going to school. Can you help me?"

So this guy, he happens to be the country director, he said, "Yes, we can help. Just write to us."

So I came back and just got paper and wrote, hand wrote an application form, you know for a partnership. That became a very interesting thing because the partnership that we did, we started with 64 children that we registered and we sent them to the schools in the community and that helped us to start helping children. And the numbers increased that were being supported. God started working because when we started helping children, the community started loving us. They felt that we were useful people after all. God used that to unlock or to break the resistance because we helped the children.

Now, in 1992, a friend of mine called Gerald Seruwaggi comes to be with me. We grew up together. I helped him and he helped me as we were growing up. But he happened to have gone to America to study. So he wrote and said he wanted to come and meet with me. Later on, he brought visitors from the states. And amongst them was a couple, Pastor and Mrs. Draper from San Antonio, Texas. These people were with us and they really liked what we were doing and we kept in touch after they left. Pastor Draper invited me to go to the states for a while.

Which is another very big story because he sent me the invitation but I didn't have the money to go. I had to trust the Lord. I prayed and I didn't have money. So I did something which was crazy, I'd never done it before was to fast and pray for a long time. Usually I would fast for a day or two days but this time I said I'm going to pray until I get a breakthrough. I went, closed my door and then stayed in prayer for five complete days without eating anything and I prayed and I had lots of challenges. Because you know, the first day when you start praying, you are hungry. The second day you get a headache because you have less water in the body. The third day you get spiritual challenges because the devil just attacks you. But those were tough days. But I remember after five days I just felt the confidence that God is answering my prayer.

So I came back and told these people God will provide for me an air ticket. Now that was a very big struggle to get an air ticket. I had two cows at the time. Not cars but cows. I said, "I can stake my cows to get money so that I can buy a ticket." No-one would buy. We had a little TV I said "I can sell my TV, add money to the money from the cows and be able to go." But we looked for someone who can buy those things. There was no money. Our church, I think for a year, the only money we could, raise in a year was probably 50 dollars or less so they could probably not come up...not probably but they couldn't come up with the money to buy a ticket. But you know God is faithful because I set the date. I wrote to my friends and I said I'm coming to the states on this day. Went and made a booking for my air ticket. But I didn't have money. So I told a few of my friends to help me get some money. Everyone had no money. I told my friends, "You are my friend, you can help me." No money.

I remember two people helped me. One of my friends introduced me to a lady in Entebbe. And this lady looked me in the face and said, "OK I think I can help you." So this lady lends me money equivalent to about $500. Now that is a Thursday and I am supposed to leave on Saturday. I take that money there to the British Airways office and it is not enough – I have to go for more money.

On Friday, another friend of mine comes to me. "I've talked to somebody; I think he might want to help. Let's go there early in the morning on Saturday." Now this is the day I am supposed to leave. So we go to this couple, they were business people in town and I tell them I have two cows and my TV. You can pay me money, and then you can keep them if I don't pay you. The guy said, "I can't help you." But just before I leave, the woman gets her husband and says, "Let's help this man." She opens the briefcase and they give me one million shillings. At that time, it was equivalent to about a thousand dollars. They give me the money and I get this money after 12. Remember this is Saturday and the airline office closes at 12:30. But the flight is at 3:00. They would put you on Uganda Airlines that would take you to Nairobi and then you get on to British Airways.

So I rush from this place, run to the British Airways office and we find them just closing. Actually they were closed but they were still inside. So we knock on the door. They open and I say I am going, here is my money. So they give me the ticket. Remember I'm in town. I can't come back to Gaba. So as we enter the British Airways office, I tell Charles, rush to Gaba and get my bag. So Charles runs to Gaba and my agent, the guy who was negotiating my ticket says I have a car – I will drive you to Entebbe. We arrive just a few minutes before the plane takes off and I fly to the states. That's how I went to the states the first time. And that is a miracle.

I ended up in Tulsa, Oklahoma. How did I end up there? A friend of mine, I had never been to the states but as we were buying tickets, my friend was going to a conference in Tulsa. The conference was at I think Roberts University. So he said, "Since you don't know the states, let's travel together." When we reached Tulsa, I didn't have any money on me.
When I reached Tulsa, I called my host and I said, "I'm here."
He said, "Where are you?"
I said, "I'm here in Oklahoma."
"Why are you in Oklahoma?" he said.
"I traveled with someone I knew and that's where I ended up."

So the guy sent me a ticket on Greyhound. He said, "Go to Greyhound Bus, you will find a ticket there." So that's how I ended up in Texas. Now that opened the whole field of America. Because I stayed in the states for four months and the church kept going here. But during that time was when I introduced the brethren that I met to this issue of child sponsorship and that's when we started our child sponsorship program and it has been going on ever since. Someone took me for lunch and he paid. I think he took me to a posh restaurant because for two of us he paid $20. And that is 93 so that was a lot of money. I said, "You know what, for that money I could get a child in school for a full month. And you just paid for just the two of us."

So this guy stands up in church on Sunday and told the people what I had told him. "Here we are in this church. We can help. From today I have decided to support a child." Other people said, "I will support a child, I will support a child, I will support a child." We ended up with 15 sponsors. So that's how we started this child sponsorship program where we now have about 800 children in the program. [January 2004 – currently the figure is well over 2000] And the Compassion program continues. With Compassion now we have about 330 kids in the program. So that's how we started.

When I returned is when I got married. That was '93 when I went to the states. We got married soon after I returned. We got married in January of '94. The first week of January '94. And that year '94, we decided to start our own school. Because we had children sponsored but we also had a challenge. Because you want to establish children in the Christian faith but we didn't have that means because there were schools everywhere. And these schools some of them were Moslem schools, some of them were pagan schools, some of them were Catholic schools. And we just felt that we needed to have our own school. So we rented buildings across the road and we started a school there. And the school has ever been growing, it's now 650 so that's how the school began and… God is amazing."

On The Road
Mark McKnight & Adam Ansel

Chapter 2

To Fill In The Gaps

Pastor Peter is an incredibly busy man. Our interview was constantly interrupted by phone calls, knocks at the door and urgent emails. I got the feeling that Peter could have talked for days about his ministry but we just ran out of time. That's why he seems to come to quite an abrupt end in his story. He is so passionate about everything he does that one cannot help but be caught up in his vision. I am convinced that he is God's man in Gaba. He is also the head of a team of able pastors, administrators, technicians, evangelists, teachers, businessmen and a whole host of other positions that make up the Africa Renewal Ministries family. Sounds cheesy, doesn't it.

Allow me to attempt to fill in the gaps. For many years, Idi Amin ran amok in Uganda and essentially decimated a once prosperous country (at least by African standards). Uganda used to be known as the 'Pearl of Africa' but it will be a long time before it is able to restore its former glory. Uganda was not entirely successful when they replaced Idi Amin in 1979. In fact, his eventual replacement, Milton Obote, was not much better. Yoweri Museveni seized power with his National Resistance Movement in 1986 and is still the president although this year's election (2006) will prove crucial. The civil war was not long finished by the time Pastor Peter started coming to Gaba. As an African, Peter tends to under-exaggerate things. Like the fact that even now it can still take an hour to travel the five or so miles to town. Or that most of the population of Gaba still live in abject poverty. Or that there are people in his church going hungry today.

They say there are about 20,000 people who live in Gaba but I fear that is over-estimating somewhat. Most of them came during the long and brutal regime of Idi Amin – the city wasn't a safe place. Gaba was a much safer place to stay although as the city has grown it has been consumed by the extending boundaries of Kampala. I have lived through civil war in my own country and I thank God that none of the children who we work with are old enough to remember these atrocities. Occasionally, someone will tell a story about when the soldiers came during the war but it tends to be very much a taboo subject.

I love Gaba. In fact, even though I have spent exactly zero days actually living there, it's the closest I have to a home. I've been thinking about running for mayor! Gaba is just a little fishing village. In the morning, it always smells of fish. We live up the hill in Kawuku, so every morning we get to take one of the most beautiful walks that I know of – down the hill, with Lake Victoria on your left and the sun rising in front of you. Wasswa and Kato, two little six year old twins used to walk with us when they saw us but I think their mom must have yelled at them because it's a long time since we've seen them. There was another little boy who had learned some English but didn't know what it meant. Our conversation would go like this...

Boy: "Mzungu [white man], how are you?"
Me: "I'm fine, how are you?"
Boy: "I'm fine, how are you?"
Me: "I'm fine, how are you?"
Boy: "I'm fine, how are you?"
Me: "I'm fine, how are you?"

I suppose we can't expect three year olds to appreciate the finer points of a language that is not their own!

Gaba Community Church has gone from a hut with a papyrus roof in 1987 with 15 members to a church that can seat 300-400 with three packed services every Sunday morning. Surrounding the church is a primary (elementary) school, a secondary (high) school, an early childhood project (nursery), a women's co-operative, two orphanages, a health clinic, an internet café, a video editing suite and various administrative offices to help the whole thing run smoothly. Take a half hour boat journey across the lake and there is a campsite where the church runs vacation bible camps, several children's homes and a primary school. There are plans for a secondary school, a conference centre and even a university – Pastor Peter has BIG dreams.

Gaba Community Church is one of the biggest buildings in Gaba. Three services every Sunday morning – all of them are packed, with people standing at the back. It holds about 300-400 people. You do the math! The early service at 8:00am is in English. The 10:00am service is in both English and Luganda (the local language – they give a translation) and the noon service is in Luganda only. Usually the girls who live with us don't make it out of bed in time for the early service so we arrive about 9:00am, just in time for the sermon and then we stay for the worship in the second service. Being a church, there's children's ministry, youth ministry, men's ministry, women's ministry, old people's ministry, prison ministry, evangelism…you get the idea. African churches sure do love to sing though. I think there are seven different choirs in the church, and that's only the official ones – there are a bunch of other informal singing groups. Especially with the children's and youth choirs, this is a great ministry to the young people who are involved – it gives them a chance to meet and fellowship with like minded people of their own age.

Mwangaza have been a choir forever. They've been singing in the church in Gaba for eight or nine years now. It seems like every church in Africa has to have their children's choir. Unfortunately, not every church has a competent musical director. I remember once we heard a children's choir in a church in Rwanda. They just seemed to repeat the same line over and over again. I'm not entirely sure there was a tune, either. It just sounded like the same note all the way through. Those kids sure were cute though. They had these nice yellow polka dot outfits. Very tasteful! During the worship, the kids were dancing with Adam and I until some lady came and yelled at them. Maybe it wasn't appropriate to disturb the shabbily dressed white visitors.

Luckily for us we have Lillian as musical director, eh? I don't think a single line repeated over and over on one note for a one and a half hour concert would have brought quite so many people to Jesus or raised so much money. It didn't inspire me much in the hour and a half we had to listen to it in Rwanda!

Years ago, someone prophesied over the Children of the Light Choir and told them that they would minister to the nations. And that's how Mwangaza started.

Jump forward a few years to December 30th, 2003 and preparations are under way to tour Texas and California with Mwangaza (meaning 'shining light' in Kiswahili), the recently renamed children's choir from Gaba Community Church, Uganda, East Africa. Setting off plenty early in the morning, Adam and I are on our way to Gaba. Basically, we have no real plans: get to know the kids, do a bit of traveling and get ready for tour.

There's something about flying, isn't there? I always seem to end up beside the weirdoes or the trouble makers. This time it was someone with a baby – the child cried throughout the entire flight. Once when I was going to America, I was sitting beside a Russian sailor. Every time the drinks cart came round he asked, "You will drink with me, no?" with his broad Russian accent. Then he would down several mini-bottles of vodka and fall back asleep. He always managed to wake up before the cart came around again. It was uncanny.

This is probably as good an opportunity as any to introduce you to some more of the cast of our tale.
James Teira is another Ugandan who I have been privileged to travel with in the past. He and I have worked together in seven different countries now – I just can't seem to get away from him! James and I have shared some of the most surreal moments of my life together. I was meant to be the best man at his wedding but then he fired me! Probably just as well – it's a pretty responsible job. James said that his parents wanted the best man to be someone who was married already. In fairness, they did offer to help me find a bride before the wedding. You have to admit though, it was rather inconsiderate of him getting married on Valentine's Day – he really messed up all our Valentine's plans!
Once when he was a boy, James ran away from home but he soon got hungry. He knew there were some mangoes on a tree outside his house so he sneaked back to steal them. Unfortunately, his dad caught him while he was still up the tree so the dad cut the tree down to teach him a lesson!
James got a job as a social worker in Gaba shortly after I arrived in Uganda for the first time. This was, of course, destiny because who should he meet in Gaba but Lillian, director of music for the Children of the Light Choir. Romance soon blossomed and just before we went on tour, James and Lillian were married.
I just heard on Valentine's Day this year that they are going to have a baby. That's something that worries me. You see, Lillian and I had a little joke that she was producing a flower girl for my wedding. She reckoned that by the time the child was three years old, it would be time for me to get married. Of course, it was all a big joke when she wasn't pregnant. But now that she is, the heat is on – I've only got about three and a half years to find myself a wife now!
(James and Lillian had a beautiful baby girl called Love Joy at the start of June 2005. The poor child – she looks just like James!)

Joshua has been involved in the technical ministry for a long time in Gaba and so he came along as one of our sound engineers. Joshua is, as we say in Ireland, a good lad. His heart is in the right place.

While we're traveling, we teach the kids so that they don't fall behind in their schooling. Auntie Sarah traveled with us to ensure that their schooling was looked after.

Finally (for now) is Adam, one of the best friends a guy could ask for. Hailing from the thriving social hub that is Cumberland, Maryland, our friendship has been bonded over In And Out Burgers, Blizzards from Dairy Queen and skateboarding. I'm a little jealous that God called him to move to Uganda before me but what can I do? Every morning I wake up and ask God, "Can I go to Africa today?" Every morning God replies, "Not yet. I have big things planned but not yet." I'm not sure if I'm not ready for Africa yet or if Africa is not ready for me.

Some of life's most important and scary moments have been shared with Adam. He had Christmas at my mom's house in Lisburn before we went to Uganda. He picked out this real nice mini-fir tree to give my mom for Christmas which we went to great lengths to hide until Christmas day. Unfortunately, the Northern Ireland winter killed it and it went to that great fir tree heaven in the land fill site!

On The Road
Mark McKnight & Adam Ansel

Chapter 3

UGANDAN PREPARATIONS

As I said before, Adam and I didn't have any real plans when we arrived in Uganda – get to know the kids, pray with them, play with them, etc. The first order of business when we arrived was to help with the recording of the album that we would sell as merchandise on tour. Marius from San Antonio had flown out especially to do the recording so we were something of a spare wheel when the kids were recording. While Marius recorded with some of the children inside the church, we did what we do best outside the church – hung out with kids, played Jenga and told stories.

I've always been amazed at Adam's ability to relate to children. If he sits down, it isn't long before he is surrounded by kids – telling them stories, asking them questions and learning their language. We used to have story telling competitions to see who could come up with the best stories on the spot, usually when it was raining and we couldn't go outside to play soccer.

Once we were round at James' house and the electricity had gone off. So we started telling stories and I began telling them the story of the Three Little Pigs. Each time the big, bad wolf said, "And I'll huff and I'll puff and I'll blow your house down," I got louder and louder. By the time it came to the house made of bricks, I said it so loud that I blew out the candle that one of the children was holding – they laughed and laughed for ages!

Marius even came around for dinner one night and we sang each other songs that we had written – that is always fun. Marius' country ballad was a big hit – something about the party never ending and the road going on and on. It's hard to beat some good old country music. Adam's a bit obsessed with it though – almost every time I got in his van on tour he was searching for the local country station. Once, the kids were complaining that they had no music to listen to so I suggested that since Uncle Adam had all kinds of music on his computer, he should burn them some CDs. Their answer was, "But Uncle, it's all country music."

In all honesty, although we were around while they were recording the album, we didn't contribute much apart from keeping the children entertained who weren't needed at that particular time. We did get free lunches most of that week though, since they provided the kids with their lunch. Almost every day we used to walk around to Kyabeeyi restaurant and have chips (fries if you're American). Except for the day they decided not to tell us when they were going so we missed lunch that day. Unfortunately, Kyabeeyi is closed down now – apparently the owners couldn't afford the rent. Adam and I were badly disappointed by that – we used to go and watch the soccer there. Once we almost got beaten up in Kyabeeyi because we were cheering for the wrong team.

Mwangaza did a really important concert while we were there – they sang for the Uganda National Youth Conference. President Museveni was meant to be there but he didn't show up until late so he didn't hear the children sing. He has heard them a couple of other times, including at the Ugandan National Stadium in front of a capacity crowd of about 15,000. The children even got their pictures taken with the president and his wife. At the youth conference, the speakers were mixed. The president's speech was brilliant – he even organized dinner for the whole conference at the drop of a hat but there was some other guy who spoke – I think he was one of the president's aides or something. We all fell asleep when he was speaking. Quite literally. I'm surprised no-one yelled at us. With our luck, they usually do!

I want to tell you about this great new diet I've found. Forget Atkins' – I lost thirty pounds in a month on the malaria diet! For some reason, which is a great irritation to me, mosquitoes just don't seem to bite Adam. Possibly for a similar reason, they seem to really like the taste of me. So (as I see from my journal), on January 21st after three weeks in Uganda, I had malaria. Now you're probably thinking that I forgot to take my tablets. Actually, I was taking the tablets and I still got sick. Once again, this is the story of how God looked after us in Africa and in America. I'm sure you've heard the stories about malaria – fevers, sweats, chills, eyes rolling back in the head, etc. For me, malaria was more of an inconvenience than a problem.

The doctor said I was the only person he had ever met who got sick while they were taking the medication that I was on (of course, no medication is 100% effective). I wasn't able to eat for a month which is why I lost so much weight. That wasn't helped much by the cook in our house – I use the word 'cook' in its loosest sense. There were other symptoms but I'm not going to write them down – they aren't the sort of thing you talk about in mixed company. But God looked after me and I wasn't bed ridden although I was very sick for a few days. The first dose of medicine they gave me wasn't strong enough so the malaria started to go away but then came back again. I took the second dose before I went on the now infamous first (and possibly last) trip to Rwanda. Once again, God took care of me when I needed him most and brought me through to the other side.

I finally got my revenge though. Now, almost two years later, Adam finally succumbed to malaria. Thank God that he too was fine.

***This next section should not be read ***
by my mom or Adam's mom

In my first book (Msimulizi: Stories for Mwangaza), I wrote a dedication to my children and one to Adam. As part of the tribute, I wrote the line, "May our moms never find out enough to make them worry." I was mostly talking about public transportation in East Africa. By the time this book is printed, they will both (hopefully) have experienced it first hand so we may not be allowed to go back to Africa.

Specifically, I'm talking about the buses. Taxis are dodgy but only travel short distances. Buses travel hundreds of miles over mountains, across deserts and through jungles. The drivers incessantly chew leaves called qat (pronounced 'chat') as they drive. Qat has a mildly narcotic effect similar to alcohol, depressing the senses and slowing reactions. Coupled with the breakneck speeds these drivers reach on winding mountain passes, it is more or less an invitation to disaster. Now add to that my body's less than serene reaction to a second higher dosage of serious medication and Adam's digestive response to our 4:00 am wake up call and you have a recipe for one of the most miserable journeys of our lives. Nigeria's booming film industry also contributed to the misery of our journey with a film about a twelve year old boy in love with a twenty eight year old girl.

Moms can start reading again

One of the highlights of these two months in Africa was visiting Lydia, the little girl who I sponsor. She showed me around her school and we were able to spend time talking and playing together. Adam was also able to visit the two children that his parents sponsor. God willing, Adam's parents will be able to visit these two children next summer.

Our single major crisis while we were in Africa stretched my faith to the limit and almost resulted in me not getting to America at all but that is a story for another chapter…

Chapter 4

VISAS

The big question as we spent the time in Uganda was our visas to go to the U.S. Not just for me but for the rest of the choir and staff. In fact the only person who wasn't going to have to worry about it was Adam. Here's the thing: American embassies don't have a very good reputation around the world. It isn't easy to get a visa to come to America. I could tell you all kinds of stories about people I know who have been refused visas but I will tell you my own story because it is the one that shows God's hand on Mwangaza and glorifies Him the most.

Way back in December of 2003, I applied for a visa to come to America for six months to work for Mwangaza. I won't lie – lying is how the whole thing started. I told them that I was just coming for a vacation. He said the reason I was being refused was that I didn't have enough money to cover my stay here. In fairness, I didn't. As soon as I left the visa interview, I heard that familiar whisper in my ear, 'Mark, you shouldn't have lied in that interview.' That was application number one.

Application number two was filed at the American embassy in Kampala. The embassy is on the road out to Gaba so we pass it nearly every day. In fact, there's a supermarket across the road from the embassy where we buy all our 'Oodles of Noodles.' I should have known it was going to be a bad day from the moment I got out of bed. When I was leaving our house, Caesar (the guard dog from hell) escaped and I had to spend about 20 minutes chasing him to get him back inside our compound. By that time, the white shirt I was wearing was filthy dirty but I was already late so had to go to my interview in a muddy shirt. This time, I was as honest and truthful as I could be about what I was going to do in America. But the man behind the counter told me that there was no point in giving me a visa until the children all had their visas.

A couple of days later, Pastor Peter went to the embassy with the kids' passports for a meeting that had been arranged with one of the consulate officials. We anticipated that after the meeting, all of the children and staff would be sent for and questioned. I remember talking to the children about how they should answer the questions and how they should behave when they were in the embassy building. But God was at work in Pastor Peter's meeting. The embassy approved all of the visas without asking to see anyone else. Every child and member of staff was given the green light to go to America. Except me.

Application number three was made the day after the children got their passports back from the embassy with their visas. I assumed it would just be a formality – the children had their visas so they just needed to rubber stamp my passport and I was ready to go. The lady was going to give it to me but then she checked with the man who had done my second interview a few days earlier. He said that another reason that he hadn't given it to me was that he wasn't able to verify the information I had presented to him about my plans after tour. By now, I was three hundred dollars down ($100 per application) and still no visa.

Even now, it is difficult for me to write about this. As humans, we naturally see the injustice and ask, why me? On that day, I was close to tears as I walked through the gates at James' house to tell the children that for the third time I had been turned down. Some of the children were absolutely crushed. I kept asking God, "Why? Why? Why?" I had presented all kinds of letters saying who I was, what I would be doing in the U.S., who would be responsible for me, when I was coming home, what I would be doing when I came home, etc. and they had once again refused me. The situation was bleak. It looked like I would be unable to go on tour. But only some of the children were crushed by the news. Not that the others didn't care. It's just they had the faith to not just believe, but to know that God had called me to be on tour with them. This third refusal was no obstacle to them.

When I arrived at James' house, the children were noisily playing outside. When I told them the news, it wasn't long until everyone was silent. James was in the house and, being a sharp sort of fellow, noticed that it had gone quiet outside. So he came out to see what had happened. His two word response sums up the simple faith that I wish I had more of. "Apply again," he said. James too knew that God wanted me on tour but I'm from a land of privilege. I don't need to have the faith that these people have, right? Wrong!

So how was I to know if this was a test from God or if he really didn't want me to go to America? Adam and I talked about this exact question every day from then on. We prayed about it several times every day – with the kids, with ourselves, with Craig, with James, with the church. With everyone in fact.

We had all kinds of weird contingency plans worked out that involved me, Adam, Craig and Pete: the Fellowship of the Visa! They would have cost a fortune too. There would have been people flying all over the world between Africa, the U.K. and America. One night as I lay in bed, I had an idea: if I didn't go to America, I could just stay in Africa – an idea that was incredibly tempting. Looking back, it's just as well we didn't go back down that path. God wasn't ready for me to live in Uganda. Matter of fact, he still isn't which is why I'm living in Yorkshire, England for now. I'm still praying for the call.

Eventually, our faith was strengthened by that of James and the children. We decided that we would make one more attempt to get my visa. Remember those three friends I keep telling you about – Adam, Craig and Pete? Well my final application only came as a result of all three friends laying themselves on the line. Before I went for it, we had our contingency plan in place and it wasn't pretty. If I was turned down for the visa, it was really going to screw up all of our plans but each one of them said, 'do it.' This was an all or nothing gamble. I would fly back to Ireland ten days earlier than planned and make one final application at the consulate in Belfast. If it paid off, we were all laughing. If it didn't I was stuck in Ireland – broke with no way to get back to Africa. Adam would have to cut short his trip to Africa and get to Texas as soon as possible but he wouldn't be able to leave for at least another month. That meant either Craig or Pete would have to get to America within the space of one or two days to build a sound system that they knew nothing about (because I had designed it) and run it for a month until Adam could get there. Neither Craig nor Pete was in a position to do that.

We were reminded of Gideon who laid his fleeces to discover God's will so we prayed simply that if I got an appointment within the time period that we needed, then we would make this one final attempt. April 1st was the absolute deadline – the sound system had to be up and running. The story starts with my journal entry from March 2nd.

Tuesday, March 2nd, 2004
Had a good chat with James today who (as always) has complete confidence in me getting a visa. I remain unconvinced...Visited kids in Gaba and they prayed for me which gave me a heap more confidence.

Wednesday, March 3rd, 2004
Finally, a glimmer of hope – Mom called when we were in Makindye to say that I had an appointment for the 22nd which doesn't mess us up too badly.

On March 7th, the Mwangaza Children's Choir did their inaugural concert to their own church. I've only experienced that kind of atmosphere two or three times in my life – the church was electric. People were on their feet dancing, the children loved performing to their own families and it was clear that the hand of God would be on these children. The saddest man in the building was me – still no visa but at least an appointment.

Adam and I spent a few days in Kenya before I flew back to London on March 15th. By the time I arrived back in London, I realized that I still had no way of getting back to Belfast – in the flurry of activity in the last month I had forgotten to book myself a flight. But eventually I made it back to Northern Ireland and began making preparations for my interview. I did manage to spend St. Patrick's Day in Ireland which was a bonus.

Anyway, after a week of preparations, I was interviewed by the same man who had done my very first interview. This time, I was telling him the truth – God wasn't going to catch me out on that one again! The interview went from bad to worse. He remembered me and gave me a real hammering about having lied to him in the first interview. He went on and on about it and then he ticked the box to say he had refused my application.

Of course, I was frantically praying in the little interview room. The choir was already in America so it was still only three in the morning in Texas. James told me that for no reason, he woke up in the middle of the night and started praying for me. Adam, Craig and the whole church in Uganda were praying for me. My church in Lisburn was praying for me. And so I gave up – I stopped praying. I was destroyed. After all our prayer and preparations it had come to a fourth refusal.

Then, something must have caught the eye of the man doing my interview. Or his attention was grabbed by something I had written. Or God gave him an almighty slap on the back of the head and told him he was making a mistake. He started to ask me questions about our organization. He asked me about the work we would be doing in America. He asked me about the work we do in Uganda. He asked me about Pastor Peter. And then he scribbled his tick from the no box and put a new one in the yes box. As simple as that. I could have cried with happiness.

> *Monday, March 22nd, 2005*
> Praise the Lord for his mercies endureth from generation to generation. I got my visa on just the fourth try...Spent the rest of the day walking on air. Well, tiling my brother's bathroom floor really. From the sublime to the ridiculous! Hallelujah!

Although this story is long and has me as the central hero, I don't include it to emphasise my own importance to the choir. Quite the opposite – I know that God only sent me to where he needed me. I learned a huge lesson in faith through all of this. It cost me $400 for my four applications – money well spent as far as I am concerned. You see, I've realized that if God wants you to be somewhere, he will move mountains to get you there but you should pay attention – you might just learn something along the way.

Part of the reason that I am writing this book is to encourage you to get involved in ministry. It doesn't have to be Africa Renewal Ministries. There are a million great ministries to get involved in. God doesn't call everyone to move to Africa. He hasn't even called me to move to Africa (yet!). But he calls people every day to do his work and if he wants you there, nothing is going to stop you – not even three refusals for a visa. All you need to do is have the faith that he can take you there.

Years ago, God called a friend of mine to China. But he had a full time job, a wife and three children. He still has the wife and three children but one of them has grown up and moved out (a child, not the wife!) and he just took early retirement. I'm excited to see God moving in his life. It's no accident that he's now unemployed so to speak. Of course, he's been taking a course in Mandarin Chinese for several years now – it doesn't hurt to be prepared. What has God been calling you to?

On The Road
Mark McKnight & Adam Ansel

Chapter 5

ARRIVING IN AMERICA

    I can't tell you much about the kids' first few hours and days in America because I wasn't with them. So I've got some of the kids to tell you in their own words. I was going to edit them but it's so much more real to read what the kids actually said. It's funny reading them and remembering some of the things that happened.

<u>Joy and Angella</u>

    We left from Gaba at four in the afternoon and reached Entebbe. We checked in our luggage and then afterwards we boarded the plane at seven. When we reached Nairobi one hour later we had dinner and then we boarded another plane to London, England. We were in London for three hours, some people were vomiting and everyone was very tired. The plane in London was delayed and we missed the flight to Chicago. When we reached Chicago we were so tired that we couldn't even walk. We slept at the airport since we had missed the plane. They gave us free food from McDonald's at the airport. Uncle James woke us up, when they woke up Dwayne he walked far away from us and Uncle James started looking for him, we were all scared. Dwayne was found far away sleeping. Then we boarded the next plane, everyone slept on that plane. We reached Texas and found there many people waiting for us like Mama Dana, Aunt Cheryl, and many others.

On The Road
Mark McKnight & Adam Ansel

Once we got our luggage we went to the cars. We all got into different cars, Angella was sick and Joy was tired. When we went to the Player's House we saw the roads were so nice. We thought America was more developed than Uganda with nicer roads, cars, and buildings. The buildings were so big and cute!

Then we reached the Player's House. We entered and found Uncle Brian and Aunt Courtney. The Player's House was like a hotel for people to stay. We were introduced to many people and then we went to shower and slept.

The next morning we woke up and we had showers. They gave us clothes and we went for games. Megan took us. We played with hula-hoops.

We thought that in America there was no soil, but we found soil there, there was too much grass.

The first day was boring because we were missing our parents and our friends back in Uganda. The food was so different like pizza, and we ate too many vegetables and vitamins which we didn't like. But we had to get used to the situation.

The second day we went for practice at Wayside Chapel. By the time we reached it was cold and we weren't used to the weather. Many children were sick: Joy, Jesca, Angella, Ponsiano, most of them.

The people were nice, they treated us so good. We used to get families that came to visit us and they would bring us food, clothes, and other things. Some of the children's sponsors came to visit us while we were staying at the Player's House. Like Jackie, Angella, Ponsiano, and Freedom.

We would do devotions in the morning and again in the evenings. There was a lady who would come to teach us and she told us a funny story about a dog.

After practice we would have school at Wayside Chapel. The second day we were there we learned the Star-Spangled Banner. It was cool, we like it, but it was very hard to learn.

Tana and Megan would teach us English and we would have a lot of fun.

We really enjoyed the Player's House because it was cool.

In the Player's House we had different rooms with different colors: Yellow room, Red room, Blue Room, and Tan Room. The Red room was for boys and the others were for girls. Uncle James and Auntie Lillian had their own room but the others stayed with us children.

There was a lady, Auntie Joanna who invited us to her home and that was our first day to eat hot dogs and marshmallows. We also painted hard-boiled eggs.

Ponsiano

    The day we left from Uganda it was a good day. We went very early but we arrived very late. It was a very big experience in all the planes, but especially the last plane because for me my side all the planes I was not feeling sick but the last plane, I don't know what happened but I started to get sick. I think because I ate a lot. When we got off the plane I was becoming very dizzy because of being tired and they asked us whether we wanted to board a plane or a train, but we refused to board the plane because all of us were sick and we didn't want to walk any more we just wanted to stand on the elevators. The American airports were very big that every time we would walk our legs were just paining.

    When we arrived it was night and when we went through customs we found people raising up banners and they said, "Mwangaza." There was Cheryl, Auntie Marci, Tana, and Betsy. They welcomed us and they divided us to go in pairs to go to the Player's House.

    For me Auntie Cheryl took me and others. When we arrived we were so tired that I didn't even want to eat anything. I didn't like the American water because it was somehow salty. When you took it, it wasn't the same as Ugandan water. When they showed us the showers the first time some of us didn't how to use them and they didn't know how to shift the cold water and the hot water. The first days water could burn us and sometimes the water was very cold, but by time it was going well.

    At Wayside the first meal we had we didn't like because it was smelling in a way that we didn't know and it was a very big experience for us. When we were doing practices, the first week we were in America, I got sick. First it became like flu and later I started vomiting without telling anyone that I was vomiting, but what showed me I was sick was when I was in Cheryl's car then I vomited and Cheryl told the other people that I was sick. Then they started packing me with drugs.

    American flu was very terrible. My nose started getting wounds were I was sneezing. In time I got well.

    The first days at Player's House I didn't like the breakfast because in Africa we were used to taking hot tea not cold milk and cold bananas. The first days the cereal and milk was my favorite breakfast because I could mix and I had variety.

    When we started going to Wayside for practices it was a very big experience and exciting. We saw many cars parking at the yard waiting for us. Everyone could go in a car they felt like and we started seeing new models from the cars which were coming to take us. The people who drove us were very exciting. There was an

Auntie staying with us at the Player's House and she used to put very good music on in her car. It was loud! We liked that a lot.

Our first Sundays when we went to Pastor Draper's church we liked it a lot. In the other churches like Wayside and other American churches they could not dance a lot like we wanted and they could not enjoy, but when we went to Maranatha it was like we were at home. We saw people shouting and I saw there a Ugandan whom I know. He was playing keyboard.

When we went from the airport I felt like we were driving on the wrong side of the road. I was seeing all the people driving on that side. Where we were staying at Player's House they had two gateways. One for coming in and one for getting out. But the surprising thing was when we arrived I didn't see where we passed because it was night, but in the morning I thought that we were going to pass the right direction but eventually I saw the car branching the other side and I thought they just planned it. Coming back they passed again the wrong direction.

Another interesting thing was the first week everyone was playing their own games but when I had some free time I went on the keyboard and all along I had seen many keyboards on TV which don't have power and I never knew that there were keyboards without power. I had seen them but I didn't know. [Talking about a piano] I went in a church somewhere and the keyboard was there but I didn't take time to see whether there was electricity but at Player's House, the keyboard which was there was just using strings and it was cool. We could play wherever we wanted because you wouldn't fear about it breaking without electricity. It was a very good experience for me.

The first week we had a problem of waking up very early even before it was morning because our brains had a fixed time and it took us a very long time to get used to the time. It was midnight and our brains were awake and we couldn't sleep anymore, we could talk until daytime. When they gave us some pills to help us sleep it didn't work because we were still waking up at the same time. It was a very big experience.

William Kigozi

We flew from Entebbe to Nairobi that was a one hour flight. We reached there at night and we had dinner at the restaurant. After that we had to go get the tickets and then we boarded the plane from Nairobi to London. That was a seven hour flight. We flew from London to Chicago. In Chicago we had dinner and ice cream. All of us were very tired. Dwayne was so tired he started walking in the airport and was almost lost. Uncle James looked for him and after getting Dwayne we boarded the plane from Chicago to San Antonio.

We reached San Antonio airport around twelve midnight. At the airport we found Mommy Dana, Tana, and other guys waiting for us with very big cards saying, "Mwangaza you are welcome!" Then we drove to the Player's House. We had some drinks when we reached and then the boys were taken to their room and they showed us where everyone was supposed to sleep. On the beds we found our names written plus a journal book.

First of all the people we met at the airport were very friendly and polite and lovely. The roads in America were very good there's not a lot of traffic. Their food was good but at first we did not like it. When we went on we got used to it.

When it reached morning we went for devotions and we played some games. We had many visitors who came every day. Our first church to go to was Wayside Chapel. We had school there. When we went to Wayside Chapel we had practice with the King's Kids choir. That's where we had our first concert.

Before Uncle Mark came we were waiting for him and when he arrived he had King Solomon and two bags. We were very happy to have him. When Uncle Mark came he was given a room with the boys. He brought a Gameboy with him and the boys would play with it when he was not there. Then Uncle James found us.

We went to a very small church where the youth would gather and we listened to music. We sang with those guys and they were good friends to us.

On The Road
Mark McKnight & Adam Ansel

Chapter 6

FINALLY I ARRIVE

I had my visa interview on the Monday. The passport was meant to arrive in Tuesday's post before noon. But noon came and went with no passport. I was due to fly on Wednesday morning so there was no margin for error. 12:15pm the postman arrived with passport in hand. I have never been so happy to see the postman. And on the Wednesday morning I once again hit the road. Here's my journal entry...

> *Wednesday, 24th March, 2004*
> Set out from Lisburn on this new adventure at 7:00am, arrived at midnight – 23 hrs traveling. Baggage searched twice en route and a fairly lengthy personal search in Houston. Of course, that is not to mention the immigration official questioning my visa. How heartbreaking – to suffer all of the above and fall at the last hurdle. But the guy let me go. Once again by the grace of God. Stood in Houston airport marveling at Starbuck's, Taco Bell, Popeye's et al. Just thinking about all that fantasizing Adam and I did as we lay on the living room floor after one of Irene's 'dinners.'

Let me explain – when we were in Africa that was our tactic to keep the food down. Once we had finished eating, we would lie on Craig's living room floor and talk about all the junk food we were going to eat when we got to America. You see, we had just got a new house girl and she was so bad that we had to send her on a cooking course. She used to produce this soggy rice that was all but inedible. Every time we went shopping, she insisted that we bought this stuff called Royco which was, apparently, essential for cooking. We still aren't quite sure what it tastes like since no two meals were the same! Still, beggars can't be choosers. Poor Irene – we had to fire her in the end. We used to have a pet dog called Candy. The kids came home early from school one day and found that Irene had poisoned poor Candy. It's lucky all dogs go to heaven.

I digress. Back to the airport. The immigration official looked at my passport, went and checked with his supervisor, asked me a bunch of questions and shook his head quite a bit. I don't need to tell you that when an immigration official is shaking his head, it's not a good sign. But as I wrote in my journal, "once again, by the grace of God." Even now, it is honestly a miracle to me that I ever made it to America. For 3 months before I got there, it seemed to get less and less likely that I would get there and even at the last moment there was a problem. But I can testify that he's an on-time God. Oh, remember when I'd been turned down in Uganda and I was ready to give up? Finally, having gone through immigration in Houston, I understood. God actually wanted me in America, on tour with these kids.

Essentially, I'm a very stupid person. I love reading about Peter because he's just so daft. So impulsive. So stupid. It makes me think that there's yet hope for me. He always seemed to get a bit mixed up. All the sermons I've listened about Peter walking on the water talked about Peter sinking because he took his eyes of Jesus. But just think of those first two steps while he still had his eyes on Jesus. Go Peter! I see myself as much more of a Peter than a Philip. Remember in Acts 8 when Philip explained Isaiah's prophecy to the Ethiopian eunuch? An angel of the Lord tells Philip where to go and Philip just goes. He left a successful ministry just like that.

Now read Acts 10: 9-23 where Peter has his vision about clean and unclean foods. That's the passage that gives me real hope. You see, God knew that Peter was daft as a post so he gave Peter the same vision three times in a row and then sent three dudes to come and fetch him. The rock on which Jesus builds his church and he's dumber than a sack of hammers. I love it.

So I like to picture Jesus meeting me just on the other side of passport control at Houston airport. Our conversation would go something like this:

Jesus: Mark, you're just on time. OK, let's get to work.
Mark: Just on time? There was a while there when I didn't think I would make it.
Jesus: What do you mean?
Mark: Well, all that stuff with the visas.
Jesus: But you knew that I needed you here in America. Why didn't you have faith that I would bring you here?
Mark: Well, all those times I got turned down for my visa. I was losing faith a bit.
Jesus: But James told you that God needed you on this tour. So did Adam. And the kids. And Dana. And Pastor Peter. Wasn't that enough for you?

Finally, I catch on to the fact that God really did want me in America on this tour. Like I say, I'm more of a Peter than a Philip.

The kids went crazy when I arrived. We had already passed through so much together and the tour hadn't even started yet. But when Jesus said, 'let's get to work,' he meant it. I had about one week to piece together the sound, lighting and video system that I had designed - a job that could easily have taken two weeks if things didn't go according to plan.

Now is as good a time as any to introduce you to almost all of the rest of the players in our little tale. San Antonio, Texas is the U.S. base of operations of Africa Renewal Ministries. Although there have been major changes since then, at the time the board consisted of David and Dana Mann, Tom Brown, Mike Gauntt and Brian McKinney (from California). Tom's wife, Bonnie and Mike's wife Kim were also key players back in the beginning.

David and Dana are Texans born and bred. They are some of the nicest people I know. They keep inviting me to go hunting with them but I just can't seem to manage to get to Texas during hunting season. Once they let me sleep on their sofa and that was before they had even met me.

Tom and Bonnie Brown live on a street called Mossy Cup which I think is one of the best street names I have ever heard. I don't really know what Tom does for a living – something to do with investment which I don't understand. He has a nice office though where he watches share prices on cable TV while he works. I have a lot of respect for Tom and Bonnie. As we say in Ireland, they aren't afraid to call a spade a spade. They too put me up in their home and Tom even taught the boys how to turn wood and supplied us with hand made drumsticks for the tour.

Mike and Kim are from Boernie, Texas. I have no idea what Mike does for a living. Maybe I should ask him some day. Mike is cool. He yelled at Adam and me once when we were being naughty boys but I better not tell you that story – we learned our lesson! I don't think I ever stayed in Mike and Kim's house.

I want to give a really big up to the board wives here – Dana, Bonnie and Kim. I don't mean this in any sexist way because they did all kinds of other things too but they were like the tour moms. They cooked breakfast for us, helped with the washing, made sure we all had clothes, told us what we needed to bring when we were leaving the house, etc. David and Dana were the only board members who had the chance to spend any time touring with us which was a shame – maybe the rest will spend some time on the next tour.

The board also included Brian McKinney from Simi Valley, California. He works for an organization called Children's Hunger Fund and is one of the wisest men I know bar none. Brian is one of the greatest assets that our organization possesses – he is a skilled diplomat, administrator and most importantly a great advocate for our cause.

Let's revise the roster of touring staff and introduce a few new names. James and Lillian, Sarah and Joshua all traveled from Uganda with the children. And of course there's the wee man from Belfast.

Next to boost our numbers was the Klemcke family, all from San Antonio. Marci, the head of the family, signed up to be our tour leader. If she'd known what she was letting herself in for, she might not have volunteered. But I want to write this here in print, specifically to encourage Marci because I know she'll read it. Although we had our disagreements, we could not have done the tour without Marci. Marci, two thumbs way up for you. Pray for Marci. She has teenagers! Just kidding. Marci brought her entire family on tour. Tana is the teenager. Sixteen during tour but (as I'm sure she would be at pains to point out) she is eighteen at the time of writing. Tana was in charge of all our merchandise – CDs, T-shirts, African crafts, etc. She did a really good job of it too. Of course, once she had taken her cut, it worked out quite profitably for her! (That's just my little joke by the way but I'll tell you more about finances later). Kara and Corey are Marci's other two kids. Sadly, I didn't get to know them that well. They hardly ever rode on my van so we didn't talk much. We used to get in trouble with Corey quite regularly for letting him go on our skateboards. When I finally left tour, Corey gave me a card which said, 'But who will I fight with now?'

Joe David is another resident of San Antonio. He never really signed up to come on tour, he just sort of did. He was around and helped us for all the concerts in San Antonio and when we left, he just came with us. There had been some confusion about whether he would come or not. Then we were loading some stuff into the trailer one night after a concert and Tana yelled across the parking lot, "J.D., you're coming with us." I think it was more of an order than an invitation. JD is a top bloke. He was even a part of the Summer Fun experience – a co-contributor to the Pepsi shortage in Southern California.

I think that's it: our entire road team except Adam – he doesn't join us for another couple of months.

On The Road
Mark McKnight & Adam Ansel

Chapter 7

THE KIDS

As I write, I have realized that I've made no attempt to introduce you to the children. As they are the sole reason I do what I do, I will take this opportunity to introduce you to each one of them and maybe tell you some funny stories about them. When I wrote my first book, I got into trouble for writing bad things about them so I shall be careful what I write. At the outset, know that I love each and every one of them individually, as will you if you have the privilege to meet them.

Let me start with my boys. They were boys back then but every time I see them, they have grown further towards the men of God that I pray they will become.

Dwayne was the baby of the boys. He was a few years younger than the rest and he was always trying to keep up with the bigger boys. One night he ran across the room to hug me when I wasn't expecting it. He jumped on to my lap but his head arrived first and broke my nose. Dwayne lived for swimming. If there was a pool in the host family, there was no point trying to get him to do any homework. That was fine by me, since I lived for swimming too.

Freedom spent the whole tour smiling. I don't think I ever once saw him without a smile on his face. He loved to drum – as soon as he got behind a drum, his smile got even bigger. And what a brilliant name, eh? He lives right around the corner from us now so half the time he doesn't bother going home at night – he just falls asleep on our sofa.

Malachi was one of our two proper soccer players. The others liked to play but Malachi could really play. His dad used to play for the Ugandan national team. We went in one host family and they had this neighbor who played soccer. He was good and he knew it – he liked to tell people how good he was. Until he played against Malachi, that is. The kid had no idea how Malachi was beating him – he couldn't even see where the ball had gone most of the time! I was so proud of my boys that night. Malachi was always playing with the kids from the host family. He was truly an ambassador for our organization.

Nicolas was in the middle and loved fast cars. Larry and Meredith (see host families chapter below) took us to some of the car dealerships one night and he was in seventh heaven. I remember one host family who had a yellow mustang that they took us riding in – he really loved that car. The biggest smile I have ever seen on Nicolas' face was the day he met Kirk Franklin (see below). Nicolas was a huge soccer fan although he preferred watching it to playing it. He was always asking Adam and me to check the English Premiership results for him. Nicolas hated two things in life: swimming and pizza. So when we went to a pool party where they served pizza, he was just miserable. One of his best friends' uncle runs a movie theatre of sorts in Gaba (it's a room with a TV). They are always showing soccer games and since we are basically part of the family, we always get in for free.

William is quite simply one of the goofiest people I know. I loved every minute of touring with William, even though he did have a talent of attracting trouble. If something was happening, you could usually be assured that William was in the thick of it. But he worked so hard in school – every night in the host family he would be working on his homework, which was unfortunate when he went in the host family with Dwayne and I.

Martin was our other soccer player. He could literally play rings around Adam, James and me. On the soccer field and in life, Martin was very passionate which got him into trouble once or twice. He was also a teenager and hormones were kicking in like there was no tomorrow! These days, he's doing well in school. He works hard and gets good grades. We know his mom quite well (she runs one of the children's homes in Gaba) so we always hear how he is doing at boarding school.

Lastly among the boys was Ponsiano. Ponsiano was the biggest boy and the one who I really bonded with. We used to have huge arguments with each other about all kinds of things but he is very close to my heart. We worked with another boy called Derrick who Adam always felt he had a special parental responsibility over and I never understood what he was talking about until I toured with Ponsiano. Once, when we were talking about reading the bible, James told the boys they shouldn't read from Song of Songs – he didn't want the boys' hormones to get any extra encouragement on tour! So, not wanting to disobey his Uncle James but interested to know what the book was about, he asked me during devotions in the host family one night to tell him about it. He was so funny – he always seemed to end up going to the host families that had pretty teenage daughters. No such luck on my count – I was always praying for a host family with a twenty something daughter but it just never happened. That was probably God's way of keeping me out of trouble!

I had an entirely different relationship with the girls than the boys. Since I only went in the host family with boys (for obvious reasons), I felt a special responsibility for them. I could enjoy myself a little more with the girls. Of course, I've always felt that boys are better than girls. No, seriously – it was even in the newspapers last week. The headline said "Boys are Better Than Girls" and the tagline said "Girls: They Smell and have Cooties!" He he he!

Daphine was our smallest girl and was simply a joy to travel with. She used to hang out with Kara all day – they would do their own thing and never really cause any trouble. I think they really miss each other now that they are thousands of miles apart. I don't think I had to yell at Daphine once in the whole tour which is more than can be said for some of the other kids! Daphine always struck me as a very independent person and didn't really talk to me much – only if she needed something or if she wanted some help. When I had to leave tour early, I wasn't prepared for how upset the children would be but Daphine's tears really touched me. I know a little of her background and she practically raised herself – she's one of the kids I'm so desperate to help when I go to Africa.

Leah was another goofball of the tour. In eight months of Africa and tour, I took something like six thousand photographs on my digital camera and a significant proportion of those are of Leah pulling silly faces. Sometimes she didn't even realize she was doing it – she'd just sit at the dinner table looking at herself in a spoon and making funny faces. We used to sing 'Sugar Sugar' by The Archies to her. She thought it was cute that we changed it and sang "Ooooh Leah, Leah. You are my candy girl..."

Cissy used to make me laugh every time I looked at her. She has these chubby cheeks and she hates it when you squeeze them. Cissy contributed to a great deal of coldness in my life.

When we got out of the swimming pool, she was always cold so she'd borrow my towel and leave me to sit in the cold. I don't think I ever saw Cissy without a smile on her face. She was truly a joy to travel with.

Jackie was the most grown up young girl I've ever seen. I interviewed Leah, Cissy, Daphine and Jackie for a project I was working on a long time ago before we even went on tour. The other three girls were just playing but Jackie was all business. She kept saying, "You people, we need to get serious now." Mostly, the four girls just argued about who was going to answer the next question. Jackie was another one of those kids who was a joy to travel with. She has such a sweet spirit. When she sat on my van, she was always helping out to clean it. When we stopped for gas, she would clean my windscreen and mirrors for me.

Dorothy A traveled on my van for most of the tour and she was another joy to travel with. One day last Christmas I met her in Gaba and she demanded that I come home with her to meet her mother. I'm not speaking out of place because I know she would freely admit this but when Dorothy came on tour, she was scared of almost anything. One of my happiest days on tour was when Dorothy finally jumped in the water and swam without any fear. To begin with, she was too scared to even get in the water. James didn't help matters much – his method of teaching someone to swim is to throw them in a swimming pool. It honestly took me months to get Dorothy to swim. By the end of tour, she was diving and everything. It was such a blessing to see Dorothy come out of her shell over the few months I traveled with her and see her get over some of her fears. Another thing that Dorothy was scared of was roller coasters and fairground rides. We had been to Sea World and Six Flags in San Antonio and mostly Dorothy was too scared to get on the rides but with Adam and me holding her hand, we managed to convince her to go on a ride at Kemah Boardwalk near Houston. On the first ride, Dorothy screamed the whole time, keeping her eyes tightly shut. When we got off, tears were streaming from her eyes but her first question was, "Can we go again?"

Dorothy N had the cutest giggle. Some days she would carry the weight of the world on her shoulders but when she laughed, everyone around her would laugh too. Dorothy loved to have her photograph taken. The kids used to borrow my camera and when I got it back, there would be lots of pictures of Dorothy modeling for pictures – she had all the moves and poses worked out!

Gladys used to sit on my van with the two Dorothys and was probably the child who ministered to me most on the tour. For one so young, she was such an encourager – when times got tough, as they often did on tour, Gladys would be there to give you an encouraging word right when you needed it. I think she actually understood that I'm a flawed person but that God loves me anyway. She was another beautiful spirit to have on the tour.

Angella N is Leah's big sister and so she was always looking out for her little sister. Angella and I kept having to go to the doctor together – she used to have big problems with her eyes so she would tell me all kinds of stories while we were in the waiting room. She was and is a very determined person. I am sure that Angella will accomplish great things in her life. When I left tour, her card said, 'Thanks for standing in mom and dad's gap.'

Angella M was another very independent girl. She is very intelligent and usually places very close to the top of her class. All of her family are very talented singers so when we're working on a project or a demo when we need some vocals, Angella and her sisters are always the first people who are called. It doesn't help that they live almost next door to the church! I used to tease Angella about how many solos she sang in the concert but she is a very talented young lady and I hope that tour has encouraged her to greater things.

Priscilla, in some ways, was one of the most mature girls in the choir. She and Tana really bonded with one another. I remember the night before we went to Disneyland, the two of them sat up late braiding each other's hair. Another incredible singer and dancer, she was a real asset to the choir and really ministered to people during the concerts.

Joy is Angella's big sister, although she's shorter and a bit quieter. I'm sure that Joy will become a pastor some day – she has a real heart for ministry and I know that she ministered to me and many of the other members of staff throughout the tour. Joy was everyone's big sister and she was always encouraging them to do the right thing and to look after one another – it was such a joy (no pun intended) to watch her grow and mature during the tour.

Omega is Jesca's little sister and was simply a sweet child to travel with. Omega was in the middle of the girls – not quite young enough to hang with the little kids and not quite old enough to hang with the older girls. But she managed – she was a joy to be around. Nowadays, she's studying hard in boarding school and getting good grades.

Jesca was the oldest girl in the choir and at seventeen could be quite a handful! She used to ride in the front on my van and we would argue all the time about what music we were going to listen to while we were traveling. Jesca is like a little sister to Adam and I – we even had to deal with the unwanted attentions of a boy once. Jesca could sing like few seventeen year olds I have ever met. We want to try to record an album of Jesca by herself – she's that good. Just one of the many projects that God has lined up for me when I eventually am allowed to return to Africa.

So that's it then – now you know the full cast list of our tour, both staff and children. These are the people that I have come to regard as my family.

Chapter 8

CONCERT DAY

WITH COMPLIMENTS

MWANGAZA

Dear Host Family,
   Please find enclosed a backstage pass for the Mwangaza Children's Choir concert taking place at your church this Friday night. The concert will begin at 7:30pm but you are welcome at the venue any time after lunch.

   Yours welcomingly,
   The Mwangaza Children's Choir

JOY DOROTHY·N PONSIANO
DOROTHY·A WILLIAM
LEAH Dwayn. Jackie Nicholas
DAPHINE. MALACIA Freedom
MARTIN angella Nakato GLADYS Cissy
ANGELLA·M Priscilla

VIP
MWANGAZA Children's Choir
BACKSTAGE PASS

On The Road
Mark McKnight & Adam Ansel

Concerts are the heart and soul of the tour. You are about to get an inside view of our concert that few people get to witness. It isn't always pretty and there are sometimes a few arguments, but I am sure the staff will be on their best behavior today since they have a visitor. You are visiting a concert in the middle of tour – at the start of the tour things often didn't run quite so smoothly.

You stand waiting in the blistering heat outside a church somewhere in deepest, darkest California. The Sunday School or King's Kids or whatever you call it has made a banner saying 'Welcome Mwangaza' and as our three white vans (two of which pull trailers) arrive in the parking lot, everyone begins cheering. The three drivers and two passengers are the only ones who get off the vans. A very tall, amiable San Antonio lady, two rather unkempt young men, one Irish, one American, who are furiously doing up buttons on their shirts to try to look presentable and a black man and woman who seem to know exactly what they are doing.

The tall lady is the first to speak. She introduces herself as Marci and explains that she is the tour leader. The black man and woman are the African chaperones and the two untidy men are the sound technicians. The technicians disappear to find the sanctuary while the rest of the group organizes which rooms the children are going to use. Finally, the two Africans return to the vans to get the children.

Children and adults seem to pour out of the vans. In all, twenty children and nine members of staff. The first trailer is opened and it is stacked high with luggage. A Hispanic guy starts throwing bags off and kids start catching them. Once they have their bags, the kids carry them inside. Some children return to carry extra luggage belonging to staff members who are already busy preparing for the concert. You can see that this is a well oiled machine. After all, they should be used to it – they do it four times a week.

As much as you want to hang out with the kids, play some games and have some fun, it is announced that the children will now have their nap. So sleeping bags are produced from the trailer and every child without any discussion lies down to have nap. You decide to have a wander around to see what else is happening.

You arrive in the sanctuary at the wrong moment. The sound technicians introduce themselves as Mark (from Ireland), Adam (from Maryland) and Joshua (from Uganda). They are just about to unload their equipment and would there be any chance you could give them a hand? With no immediate excuse, you are press ganged into helping. As they open the second trailer, you realize what you have let yourself in for. This trailer is even more packed than the first. You are unsure where they will begin – the trailer is literally packed to the roof.

But with military precision, they begin to unpack. The four of you take everything out the side door of the trailer and ferry it in to the church on dollies while the Hispanic guy and a teenage girl empty a bunch of plastic crates and boxes out of the back door.

The Irish guy explains a little bit about how they work – they go into the sanctuary first to see what they need, after all there's no point in carrying things in that they don't need. Unfortunately, he has decided that they need everything. So the trailer is quickly emptied – costumes hanging on a rail across the back, stage lights on hooks hanging from the roof. Huge orange and yellow electrical cables. Speakers, mixing desk, amps, screen, projector, drums and a bunch of boxes, racks and crates the contents of which you have no idea. As if that isn't enough, when the trailer is emptied (and I mean completely empty) the back doors of the van are opened and a few more things are carried from the luggage space back there. The Irish guy laughs and says that you've just carried in about one metric ton of equipment and thanks you for your help. Timidly, you ask if there's anything else you can do to help. You're glad when the other technician from Maryland says that they should be fine for now but if you're free after the concert, they will have to carry it all back out again. Would you be able to find some extra muscle too? You decide to try to find the youth group and get them to do it.

Once again you go for a wander, this time being much more careful what you are going to let yourself in for. You prepare an excuse to use just in case it involves heavy lifting.

In the foyer of the church, JD (the Hispanic guy) and Tana (the teenage girl) are preparing the merchandise for sale before and after the concert. They seem to have everything under control but they stop and chat, telling you a little bit about the work in Africa. James, one of the Africans is setting up a board with loads of pictures of children on it. Some of them are smiling. Most of them look miserable. He explains that these are children for whom they are seeking sponsors. He isn't set up yet but if you come back at the end of the concert, he'll get the forms filled in. He explains exactly what it means to be a sponsor, how much it costs and how important the relationship is – 'just like having another adopted child' he says.

In the church office, the tall lady is hard at work. The laptop is out and working and she is on the telephone. She seems to be alternating between her cell phone and the church telephone. There are two white children in the room with her who are trying their best to behave but not entirely succeeding.

You return to the sanctuary to see what is going on with Adam, Mark and Joshua but through the window, you see the stage and most of the aisle are in pandemonium. There are boxes and cables, equipment and lights strewn all over the church and you decide not to get involved.

In one of the other offices, you find Sarah from Uganda. She is working on the host family sheet – deciding who will go with which family. Some kids don't like dogs and some families can only take a certain number of people so it takes a while to put everyone in the right place. You sit down and help her – you know all the families so you are able to give her some help in dividing up the choir and staff amongst the host families. When Sarah has finished the host family sheet, she spends some time talking with you about the ministry in Uganda. She is a school teacher and is also in charge of the Sunday School in the church that all of these children attend.

After a while, you hear loud noises coming from the sanctuary so you go to investigate. It seems that Mark, Joshua and Adam have finished piecing together their sound system and have put some music on while they finish building their lights and video systems. As you arrive, so does James and gently suggests that since the kids are still sleeping, they should maybe turn the music down.

Soon, the music is turned off and they begin testing the system. Adam works on the lights, trying to get some moving lights to move the way he wants them and Mark works on the sound. He's says he's going to use something called pink noise and apologizes in advance. When he switches it on, you realize why – it is louder than the music and way more irritating. He explains that they sometimes use it to torture people but part of his equipment is a special computer that can use pink noise to set the system up by itself, saving him about an hour's work.

Mark is finished in five minutes and straight away, Joshua sits down and starts playing the piano. Adam gives up on his lights and he and Mark disappear to buy some soda – their job is finished for now. They collect JD and Tana on the way out and the four of them decide that instead of soda, they will take the van to Dairy Queen to get some Blizzards. They invite you to join them and when you get there, you offer to one to pay – it's the least you can do for these people who are doing so much for these kids.

When you get back, you sit outside the church on the warm sidewalk eating your blizzards. For a while, Mark and Adam argue about which is better: a Reece's Pieces Blizzard or a Butterfinger Blizzard. You can tell that this has been an ongoing discussion that will probably never come to an end.

Then they begin to tell stories about their time in Africa and you listen, eager to know more about where the children are from. They keep making jokes about Mark being Irish. These four clearly have a very close relationship.

Up until now, things have been fairly relaxed. At 5:30pm, everything seems to move up a gear and things become a little less easy going. The kids are woken from their nap and soon there are lots of bleary eyed children in the hallways – waiting to use the restroom, wash their face and get ready for the concert.

The first order of business is dinner. The ladies of our church have really gone all out – fried chicken and rice with jelly and ice cream for dessert. You've never seen kids eat chicken like this. Not only do they eat the meat – they also eat the gristle and when they're done with that, they start on the bones too. They even eat the rice with their fingers, despite the protestations of their aunties and uncles (that's what they call the members of staff that travel with them). At dinner, for the first time, you are introduced to Lillian, the choir's conductor. She's Ugandan and married to James. She has been napping with the children which is why you haven't met her before now. Lillian bans the children from having any ice cream without any real reason why so Adam is dispatched to explain to the cooks that it isn't anything personal – since they will be dancing and jumping so much, we don't let them have any milk products before they sing. We don't want it turning into butter in their stomachs!

By 5:55pm, Mark has started to shout announcements every minute: "SOUND CHECK IN FIVE MINUTES…SOUND CHECK IN FOUR MINUTES…THREE MINUTES…TWO MINUTES…ONE MINUTE…TIME FOR SOUND CHECK!" He doesn't seem to have much sympathy for those children who haven't yet finished eating.

At 6:00, all the children are on the stage ready for their sound check. Although Mark clearly has a microphone beside him that is connected to his sound system, he seems to prefer yelling at the top of his lungs. Adam scurries around pointing his lights at the children while Mark runs through a few songs, making sure everything is operating the way he wants it. James moves everything around on stage and Mark stands fuming inwardly. Afterwards, he explains that no matter what way things are set on the stage, James always moves them.

After sound check, the children are dispatched to their changing rooms to put on their costumes and get ready for the concert. There is still over an hour until the concert starts and you wonder why they need so long to get dressed.

Mark and Adam look stressed – there's a problem with their projector which, at the minute, means that they won't be able to show the DVD half way through the concert. They have forgotten an adaptor in the last church and without it they can't send the video signal to the projector. With the concert in one hour, it will be touch and go to make it to Radioshack and back in time. The alternative is to jerry rig something that may or may not work. They decide that Mark will try to make it to Radioshack and Joshua will mix sound until he gets back. Another member of the church volunteers to drive – you would go yourself but your wife needs the car to pick up her mother to bring her to the concert.

With your backstage pass, you take a walk backstage to see what is happening with the children. The first room you look in seems like a hurricane has hit – clothes and shoes everywhere. 'This must be the boys' changing room,' you think to yourself. This next room is much tidier. 'This must be the girls' changing room,' you think to yourself. The children are lined up in the most colorful costumes - purple and orange. They are in three rows and they are obviously warming their voices up ready for the concert. Their faces are shining and they all have big smiles on their faces so you leave them to finish their warm ups. Lillian makes you promise to come back at 7:00pm to participate in devotions with the children.

With fifteen minutes to kill, you wander around to the foyer and have a look at some of the merchandise the choir is selling. CDs, T-shirts and a bunch of African crafts. It's a shame there's no DVD to buy – this would be something great to be able to show some of your friends. Already, a crowd is gathering at the merchandise stall and JD and Tana are explaining that everything except the CDs and the clothing were made in Uganda. They are selling dolls that were made by the women's project in Gaba – some of them by the mothers of children who are here tonight. You have a look at the pictures on the sponsorship board and see a little boy that you would like to sponsor. James is by his table so you fill in the forms while you are waiting to go back for devotions. He gives you a welcome pack and a photo of Kikawa Judah, the little boy who you are going to sponsor.

By the time you are finished with all the paperwork, it is 7:05pm and so you rush back stage to join in with devotions. As you enter the room, the children are now standing in a circle singing at the top of their voices. They are dancing, clapping, jumping and generally doing most of the things that people don't do in your church. They actually seem to be enjoying praising God. Soon, they begin to sing slower, more worshipful songs. They all have their eyes closed. They all have their hands in the air. You can tell that these children really know what it means to worship God.

After a couple more songs, the children begin to pray. Not one by one but all at the same time. Some shouting, some whispering. Some standing up, some kneeling, some prostrate on the floor. They are praying for the people who will come to the concert – that they will come to know Jesus. They are praying for the families that they have stayed with. They pray for the church. For each other. For their staff. For a bus to travel in. For their families back home in Africa. Some of them have the sniffles or are sick so they come to the centre of the circle and they are prayed for too.

Adam slips in the door and explains to Marci and James that Mark has just called. They are stuck in traffic and aren't sure how long they will be. They need to be prepared if he doesn't get back in time that there will be no video in the middle of the concert. So James stops the praying and explains the situation. So they pray for that too. Eventually, the prayer winds down and our pastor prays for the kids and for the concert. You realize that even he has been bowled over by these kids in their devotions.

You take your seat in the sanctuary and soon the concert kicks off in a blaze of color, light and music. The kids are singing their little hearts out. Every one of them has the most incredible smile on their faces. The high energy music and dancing is infectious and it isn't long before a few people are up on their feet cheering and dancing. Once a few people are up, it isn't long before everyone is dancing.

There is no concert program so you don't know how long it will be until the end of the first half and there is still no sign of Mark returning. One child announces that this will be the last song in this half of the concert but 'Don't go away – we'll be right back!' Half way through the song, with no fuss whatsoever, Mark slips onto the stage from a side door, connects the projector with the adaptor he has just bought from Radioshack and switches it on. At the end of the song, the lights dim and the DVD plays just the way it is meant to. You catch just a hint of a self-satisfied smile on Mark's face as he leaves the stage. As he trips on his way down the stairs at the front of the stage, you just know it was God giving him a gentle nudge that it was His doing rather than Mark's!

The video is not all doom and gloom either. It speaks of how Gaba Community Church is really making a difference in the community. How their ministries reach out and help the whole community, helping not just with their physical needs but also more importantly helping them with their spiritual needs. During the video, you hear that still small voice of calm very gently telling you that one day you will go to Uganda.

When the video is over, Marci is on the stage telling you about the ministry, what they do, how they do it and how you can get involved. One of the things she mentions is a missions trip in six months time to help build an orphanage just across the lake from Gaba. You just know that you are meant to be on that trip. You bustle around for a pen to take down the website she calls out and then realize that it's already written on the sponsorship welcome pack that James gave you earlier this evening.

As the ushers collect a love offering for the organization, the children return to the stage and sing some worship songs. The children have changed into traditional costumes this time: goat skins and grass skirts. The boys wear rattles on their calves. When they finish lifting the love offering, the children begin to dance a traditional African dance. Some of the boys are drumming with all of their might. Others dance and the rattles on their legs add to the percussive rhythm of the dance. As the concert continues, the dancing becomes more and more energetic. Mark is mixing the sound now and it seems he isn't scared of loud music. Each song seems louder than the last!

Towards the end of the concert, your pastor arrives on the stage and spends some time with the children. He asks them what they want to be when they grow up. He asks them what their favorite bible verse is. Then he explains that before the concert ends, he has asked Lillian to lead the congregation in some worship so that they too can experience something of what we saw in the dressing room before the concert. Joshua sits down at the piano and once again the children begin to worship God. The audience takes their lead from the children and joins right in with the songs. The children sing some songs in their own language but it doesn't matter. You can tell that we are in the presence of God and that understanding the words isn't as important as just being there.

All too soon, the concert is finished and the children have returned to their dressing rooms to get changed. The audience is mostly fussing around the foyer at the merchandise and sponsorship tables. One or two (like you) are chatting to Marci the tour leader about joining a mission trip and helping out in any other way you can.

About twenty minutes after the concert is finished, the host families meet in the sanctuary to find out all the details they need. As you wait for Marci, in the background you can see Joshua and Adam directing the youth group what to carry out to the trailer. Mark is in the back of the trailer making sure that everything is loaded in the right order. It's clear that if they don't follow the system, it won't all fit in. JD and Tana are packing up, counting stock, counting money and filling in their paperwork. James is filling in all the paperwork for the sponsors.

Marci works her way through everything she needs to say so that you have a good time with the kids and they don't get into too much trouble! Soon, the children are waiting at the door and their names are called one by one to come to meet their families for the next couple of nights. You get to take Mark and Adam and three boys called Ponsiano, Freedom and Dwayne.

Phew! What a day. Finally, you leave church at 10:45pm. You are the last to leave the church because Mark can't leave until everything is loaded onto his trailer.

On the way home, you stop to pick up In 'n' Out Burgers as a special treat for Adam and Mark. (Sorry, wishful thinking!)

On The Road
Mark McKnight & Adam Ansel

Chapter 8a

SCHOOL DAYS

Happy to say, not all days on tour are quite so high octane as a concert day. The days we don't have a concert generally fall into one of two categories: travel days or school days (or a mixture of the two). To devote an entire chapter to travel days would be ill advised. After all, there is only so much you can write about sitting on a van, listening to music and drinking Pepsi.

Likewise, school days were similarly uneventful on the whole. It will come as no surprise to you that the children spent school days in school. Auntie Sarah is an excellent teacher (and that is why she was on tour) so she and some of the other African staff spent school days teaching our children so that they did not fall behind in their education while we were traveling.

For those of us not involved in school, it gave us a chance to catch up on all of the things that need to be done on the road: printing business cards, replacing outgrown shoes, tidying the vans and trailers, liaising with churches further down the road, keeping up to date with news back home and carrying out ongoing repairs on everything that we traveled with from our clothes to the vans to the sound system to the drums that the kids play during the concert.

Despite the fact that there was not a concert, those days often turned out to be the busiest, particularly at the start of the tour when we were still trying to get everything organized.

It was also on the non-concert days that we had a bit more time to play with the children. Lunchtime soccer was always a favorite although it had to be banned for a while because it was getting too rough and people were getting hurt!

Non-concert days also meant we arrived with the host family much earlier in the evening (around 5:30pm) which gave us much more time to spend with them, minister to them and be ministered to by them. I can honestly say that our children ministered as much on non-concert days as they did on those days when we had a concert. It also gave us time to go to the park, to watch a basketball game, to go to some batting cages or just play some ball in the host family's back yard – things that made us feel every now and then like we had a normal life.

Read on to find out some of the things we got up to in the host family and some of the best and worst host families we ever had…

Chapter 9

Host Families

Maximum Oh Zoh is due to all of the host families that have taken us into their homes. There is absolutely nothing I can say to express the gratitude that I know the children, touring staff and our entire team feel towards each and every person who has opened their lives to us and made us feel at home in a strange land. I'm sure the bible has a great deal to say on this subject but being a bad person, I don't know where it is. If you have any suggestions for an appropriate verse, you can let me know.

Thank you, thank you, thank you, thank you. But there's a proviso. I am thankful to everyone who took me in, but there sure are some weirdoes out there.

A book about tour would be incomplete if I did not write a chapter on the host families who took us in. When we arrive at a new church, Sarah and/or Marci were in charge of the infamous host family sheet. It was their job to distribute the children and staff out amongst the families who have volunteered to host us.

I will expound my theories on reading the host family sheet, culled from years of experience at reading them. You can tell a great deal from just the addresses. Number one is the zip code. If everyone else has the same zip code and yours is different, it means you're going to be living miles away from the church. Once, when we were in Alaska, everyone else lived in a single block around the church. Except for me, of course. It was a 45 minute drive to my house. After about 20 minutes, we turned onto a logging road so I thought, 'We must be almost there by now.' I'm afraid not – another 25 minutes along the logging road before we arrived at their house. There was a plus side to it though – they had their own lake which they let us go canoeing on. They even had a pure bred Arctic wolf as a pet.

The next thing to read on the host family sheet is the name of the street. This one is fairly simple – if you live on Cherry Blossom Boulevard, chances are it's a nice house. If you live on East 115th Street, it might not be so nice. But nice houses are a poor indicator of the quality of a host family. Some of the best host families I've stayed with live in musty one bedroom apartments. Some of the worst live in mansions. But there's a way to find out whether a host family will be good or bad and it only works the moment you walk through their door. Compliment them on their house. That's it. Say something like, "This is a really nice house you have here." Don't lie of course, but their response in that crucial moment will tell you a great deal.

People fall into two groups. The first group says, "Oh, thanks. You know we've just remodeled," or something along those lines. That's the bad host family. The second group is the good host family and you'll see why. They always say something along the lines of, "Well thanks, you know God has really blessed us with it." I guess it's about knowing where your blessings really come from. The good ones know that there is nothing they can do to deserve the nice house they are living in and by inviting us into their homes to share in their good fortune they are giving something of what they have been blessed with back to God.

There are a few stereotypes of host families to which we seem to continually be invited. Number one is Grandma and Grandpa. Their children have all grown up, moved away, got married, had their own kids, etc. They have a couple of empty bedrooms in the house now so they have the space to keep us. Now if you want to talk about breakfasts, Grandma and Grandpa are where it's at. Real proper, home cooked food: cornbread, grits, pancakes, and those four words that send a shiver down my spine: red beans and rice!

The food at our second stereotype is good for a different reason. He is, of course, Single Steve. He's a career minded, early to late thirties single guy (maybe divorced with a kid). He lives in a proper bachelor pad – always an apartment, never a house. You might have to sleep on a sofa (or even worse the dreaded air bed) but that is all made up for by the fact that he has no idea how to cook. So that means breakfast, lunch and dinner from McDonald's or some other fast food outlet. If you're really lucky, you will be in California and then you can have In And Out Burgers for every meal. Alternatively, his girlfriend might come over to cook for you – either way, food will be good. He may even take you to a basketball game.

Next is the normal family – you know, mom, dad and two or three kids. This is the one that I find the most humbling. When a child gives up their bed and sleeps on the floor so that I can have a good night's sleep. That really blows me away. I often wonder what I would do if I was inviting people into my own home. Would I give up my bed? They are always taking children to soccer practice, band practice, gymnastics, basketball games, etc. but they still find the time to look after us in their busy schedule: cooking, washing, cleaning, repairing clothes, driving us to the store. Normal family, we salute you. Maximum Oh Zoh!

So I'm sure you're just dying to hear some of the horror stories from the host families, right? There have been a few. I'll make a deal with you. I'll tell you a couple of host family horror stories but not from Mwangaza. Some of the people might be reading and then I'd be in big trouble now, mister! The other part of the deal is this. If you read the Host Family Horror Stories, you have to read the rest of the chapter – Amazing Host Family Stories. Is it a deal? And I'm going to write two amazing stories for every one horror story. That should balance things out.

Host Family Horror Stories

These may not seem so horrible to people who haven't been on tour but if you put yourself in our situation, maybe you will understand. I have two stories to make your toes curl and then four to really warm your heart.

The first story has never been personally confirmed although I have heard it from a couple of different people so it is probably true. Jay has worked on and off with us for years. When he was traveling, the choir went to this proper redneck church in Louisiana. Jay ended up by himself staying with four brothers. Now, these were the sort of guys that you sure don't want to meet on a dark night. Nonetheless, Jay climbed in the back seat of their pickup truck to go home and catch some much needed shuteye.

However, he was soon told that before they went home, they had to get rid of a corpse which was wrapped in a green tarpaulin in the back of the pickup truck. Jay thought he had accidentally stumbled into some sort Redneck Mafia family and that this night could quite possibly be his last. However, not wanting to bring the hour of his death forwards, he did what any sensible short white guy would have done in a pickup truck full of four redneck brothers who want to get rid of a body – he kept his mouth shut.

At length, the pickup stopped on top of a bridge over a wide river and Jay was asked to help move the body. Not wanting to be thrown into the waters below himself, he decided that discretion was the better part of valor and helped them throw the body off the bridge.

It was only when Jay and the four brothers got back into the pickup truck that it became apparent through conversation that the dead body was in fact that of a much loved and recently deceased family pet – a rottweiler dog. I guess we'll never know why they felt that they needed to throw it off a bridge rather than bury it in the garden!

My second story, believe it or not, also deals with animal death. Adam stayed with a host family once somewhere in America. I say that because he can't remember exactly where – not even the state. It may even have been in Canada. He does remember that it was beside a golf course but that is immaterial to the story.

The host family was an older couple: perfectly normal, articulate people. Their only quirk was a rather odd looking centerpiece on their kitchen table. For two days, Adam looked at this macabre ornament, hoping against hope that it was not what he supposed it to be: an urn. This table adornment took pride of place and was present for every meal: breakfast, lunch and dinner.

After two days, Adam could stand it no longer and very delicately inquired as to the nature of this unusual and apparently morbid dinner companion. The answer brought little comfort – this urn contained the ashes of not just one but a variety of now deceased family pets including but not limited to a dog, two cats and several rabbits.

Amazing Host Family Stories

Although I've protected the anonymity of the host families above, I feel it is OK to name and shame those host families who have gone so far above and beyond the call of duty that I have been speechless by their actions.

The first host family I want to tell you about is Larry and Meredith Freeman from San Antonio, Texas. I can honestly say that there has never been a host family I have enjoyed staying at more. It wasn't because the food was good (which it was), it wasn't that they talked with us about the best things and it wasn't that they had a huge pool with a hot tub (because they didn't). The welcome we received in their home was so heartfelt and genuine, I truly feel honored to have stayed with them. They just loved us. And I don't mean that in an 'aren't we great' way. I mean they are people who love. If you visit them, you will know what it means to love your neighbor.

One night while I was playing games with our boys upstairs, Meredith interrupted us and asked us could she wash our feet. This was one of the most humbling experiences of my life – if anything we should have been the ones washing Meredith's feet in gratitude for everything this family and all the host families did for us. The disciples too must have felt the same way when Jesus did the same for them. Larry and Meredith were some of the most genuine and godly people I have ever met on my travels. If ever someone deserved an Oh Zoh shouted from the rooftops, it is Larry and Meredith Freeman and their dog who I think was called Puppy.

Interestingly enough, the Glissons live just around the corner from the Freemans (Freemen?). The Glissons had us back to stay at their house it seems like a hundred times and we always had fun at their house. The first time there was just me and a couple of boys but one night we were desperately short of host families. So the Glissons took seven boys and four members of staff into their home at a moment's notice. Another night we had this huge water fight in the street outside their house. They even bought all seven boys a Texas Longhorns basketball strip each. Those boys looked good, all kitted out in their basketball gear.

We send each of the children home from tour with a suitcase full of things they will be able to use when they get back home. We fill them up with all kinds of clothes, school supplies, games, etc. This is partly by way of a thank you to the child for all the great work they have done furthering God's kingdom and raising money for their fellow children back home. The suitcases don't come cheap – they can cost upwards of $500 so it's a very special kind of donor who partners with us in this. But some of the most humbling stories from tour came from the Suitcase Project. It took us a while to find the 20 donors that we needed to put together a suitcase for each child. When we were running out of time, one host family came forward. They had decided that they were going to sell their car and give the money to our organization so that one of our children could get their suitcase. In all honesty, tour was a succession of people who humbled me by their generosity.

Our trip to California would not have been complete without a visit to Disneyland – what an opportunity for these children to see something truly American. Believe it or not, one host family paid for our entire touring team to visit Disneyland. Kim Gore put us up in her home the night before and the night after, paid for all our food and drinks and did everything she could to make our visit as much fun as possible. We were heartbroken that the day we went to Disneyland, she had to work and was unable to join us.

These are just a few of the many stories of host families who have amazed us by their generosity and kindness on an almost daily basis. I hope and pray that our staff and children never ever take for granted the sacrifice that many of these families make on our behalf

A year after tour has finished and a bible verse finally came to me that sums up host families from tour. It came right from the lips of Jesus. Matthew chapter 25 tells us all about Jesus separating the sheep from the goats:

> Then the King will speak to those on his right. He will say, 'My Father has blessed you. Come and take what is yours. It is the kingdom prepared for you since the world was created. I was hungry and you gave me something to eat. I was thirsty and you gave me something to drink. I was a stranger and you invited me in. I needed clothes and you gave them to me. I was sick and you took care of me. I was in prison. And you came to visit me.'
> Then the people who have done what is right will answer him. 'Lord,' they will ask, 'when did we see you hungry and feed you? When did we see you thirsty and give you something to drink? When did we see you as a stranger and invite you in? When did we see you needing clothes and give them to you? When did we see you sick or in prison and go to visit you?' The King will reply, 'What I'm about to tell you is true. Anything you did for one of the least important of these brothers of mine, you did for me.'   Matt25:34-40 (NIrV)

Some of this seems very familiar. Let's see: host families fed us when we were hungry. Check! They gave us drinks when we were thirsty. Check! We were strangers in a strange land and they took us into their homes and made us feel welcome. A bunch of host families bought or gave us clothes – both to wear and to take back to Africa (see suitcase project above). Plenty of times I was sick, the kids were sick, the rest of the staff were sick and there was always a host family there to nurse us back to health. And there was that one time that J.D. got arrested!

The good old King Jimmy Version (or the Old King Cole Bible as my friend Vicky calls it) says 'Then shall the King say unto them on his right hand, 'Come, ye blessed of my Father, inherit the kingdom prepared for you from the foundation of the world.''

So I say the same to you, our host families – Come, ye blessed of our Father, inherit the kingdom prepared for you from the foundation of the world.

I wish there was a way to repay the kindness and generosity afforded us by literally thousands of families around the world. Although I began this book with an Irish blessing, this one is just for the host families.

May God grant you many years to live,
For sure he must be knowing,
The earth has angels all too few
And Heaven is overflowing.

Go mbeannai Dia duit
(May God Bless You)

On The Road
Mark McKnight & Adam Ansel

Chapter 10

TEXAS

Africa Renewal Ministries has a few 'home' churches in America: Wayside Chapel in San Antonio, Community Bible Church in San Antonio, Maranatha Bible Church in San Antonio and Cornerstone Church in Simi Valley. That's not to say that other churches haven't been more than generous but these churches have been involved with the organization for many years and have gone many miles further than they have been asked. Let me give a big Oh Zoh to our 'home' churches first.

Straight after our arrival in the US, Wayside Chapel became our base of operations for a good two weeks while we got ourselves organized to start touring. Wayside is Tom Brown's home church so we had everything we could have asked for.

Allow me to tell you about the people of Wayside. Pastor Tim is a real man of God and has been incredibly generous in supporting our ministry with his time, his church's resources and their facilities. It seemed like if we had nowhere to go for school one day, there was always a room free at Wayside.

Next in importance, as far as Mwangaza is concerned, Laureen directs their children's choir but she has traveled to Uganda several times to work with Lillian in training our children.

During the preparations for the tour, Laureen organized for the Wayside children's choir to become prayer partners with our children months before we actually arrived in America. They traded photos and spent several months praying for one another before the tour began. It was a really special moment when they finally got to meet each other. One of our first concerts was a joint performance between the two choirs for which some of the children even traded uniforms. These friendships have lasted and some of the children continue to communicate via email

You know, now that I think about it, the technical team helped me out of a spot on several occasions when something was lost, broken or hadn't been ordered with the rest of the equipment (my fault!). Maximum Oh-Zoh for Mike and Daryn for saving my bacon on more than one occasion.

Community Bible Church (or CBC as it will hereafter be known) was a different kind of church. For a start, it was so huge that I kept getting lost in the corridors. David and Dana are involved with CBC but we also have a huge number of friends there.

All the children that we traveled with have sponsors and a good number of these go to CBC. One of the sponsors is our good friend Cheryl Stephens. In fact, she's not just any sponsor – she's in charge of the US end of the sponsorship program. Cheryl does an incredible job for such a thankless task. She also didn't complain when I took over her garage for several months with all the boxes from our sound equipment.

Cheryl sponsors Ponsiano, the biggest boy in the choir. One day, Ponsiano and I were out walking and out of the blue, he turned to me and said, "Uncle Mark, I'm really glad that Auntie Cheryl is my sponsor." It was such a sweet thing to say and it really blessed Cheryl when she heard about it. I can't recommend sponsoring a child highly enough.

On Easter Sunday, CBC had their service at the Alamo Dome (where the Spurs used to play). Mwangaza were privileged to sing on stage with their musicians and choirs. I have a bit of a tradition of always wearing a suit on Christmas Day and Easter Sunday. The kids went bananas when they saw me in a suit – they were used to seeing my old, beat up trainers and a worn out pair of shorts.

CBC was another church that we seemed to return to every week or so to do school or to host families. We even slept overnight on the floor the night before we went to Nashville for the Dove Awards (see chapter 13).

Maranatha Bible Church was our third 'home away from home' in San Antonio. The two schools in Gaba are named after this church so I had been looking forward to visiting and I wasn't disappointed. There used to be a time when Adam and I would get yelled at in every black church we went to. Maranatha was the church that bucked the trend. Maranatha isn't really a black church as such – it's a little complicated to explain. Maybe you should visit to see for yourself.

Pastor Rander Draper has been involved with Africa Renewal Ministries forever. He and his wife have given so much of themselves to the ministry in Uganda it simply astounds me. On my first Sunday morning in America, we all went over to Maranatha in the vans. It was clean on the other side of the city so it took us an hour to make it and it rained all the way there.

Honestly, on that Sunday morning, I heard one of the best sermons I have heard in an awfully long time. Pastor Draper is a true man of God and is passionate about his congregation's walk even including what they eat (that's what his sermon was about). During the service, all of our staff and children were called up to the front and prayed for. The entire congregation were then on their feet, greeting us, hugging us and generally being a blessing and a confirmation that we were doing God's work.

Between Sunday morning services, we always try to make excuses to avoid joining in the Sunday School classes. When it became clear that our excuses weren't working, we reluctantly went to the single men's class. Joshua and I were welcomed with open arms – what a change to the indifference we usually are greeted with in most other churches.

Our time at Maranatha was such a blessing and there are a few individuals who should step forward to take their bows. Leisha Brown deserves a medal, a ticker tape parade and the whole nine yards for all the work she did sorting out host families for us. Even taking us into her own home when she was stuck. Her two kids, Nate and Sharnae, were always hanging out with ours and getting each other into trouble. Elizabeth Mascorro was also there in our time of need on more than one occasion.

One of the saddest moments of tour happened while we were at Maranatha. After a long fight with cancer, Malachi's sponsor was finally called home. By the grace of God, Malachi was present at the funeral and although there were tears, the gathered saints saw how important this relationship between child and sponsor really is – this adopted son was there to pay his respects too. Praise God that a grieving widow decided to continue Malachi's sponsorship.

The one thing I really love about singing at black churches is the food in general and cornbread specifically and I was not let down by Maranatha! Larry and Meredith Freeman, officially my best host family ever, were also from Maranatha.

Having drawn your attention to these three major churches in San Antonio, don't feel that they were the only churches we visited while in Texas. We spent time in Austin, Houston, Dallas and what we in Ireland refer to as 'a bunch of little holes in the hedge.' We played in dance halls, school cafeterias, colleges, golf clubs, traditional churches, modern churches, Hispanic churches, big churches, little churches and everything in between. To finish this chapter, let me tell you a couple of funny stories about Texas...

One church we sang in, not far outside San Antonio had 800 seats. The strange part of it was that there were only 600 people living in the city. At least they have a big vision!

It was in Texas that Dwayne managed to break my nose. He hadn't seen me all day so when I came in the door and sat down, he ran across the room to hug me. He jumped head first and his head was the first thing to unfortunately connect with my nose. Luckily it wasn't bad enough to necessitate a visit to A&E.

In the whole tour, San Antonio was the only place where we actually washed the vans properly. Since there were three of them, even getting the oil changed took most of an afternoon. Washing them was an all day affair – a luxury that we didn't often have.

Chapter 11

CALIFORNIA

The journey from San Antonio to Simi Valley was an epic of monumental proportions. Just moving the choir across town is like mobilizing an army so to go right across the country was quite an undertaking. In the first stage of the trip, we made it to the Texas border and stopped to do concerts in El Paso and Las Cruces, NM. It was interesting driving along the Rio Grande and explaining to our children the significance of the river as the divide between Texas and Mexico, a natural barrier between the U.S. and its neighbor.

On the drive through New Mexico, we decided that since we were so close to the Grand Canyon, we should seize the opportunity to show it to the children. It was a major detour which added another two days to the journey and had us staying in some crummy hotels and eating in some crummier pizza restaurants. By the time we made it to the Grand Canyon, the children were in foul form. They had complained most of the way there that day and just didn't want to see it. They were still complaining as we drove into the parking lot.

As I swung my van round a corner and the Canyon came into view, silence suddenly fell over my van. I left them to their thoughts but soon a voice whispered from the back, "Is it real or is it a picture?" We had a really fun day goofing off, taking photos and enjoying being friends for once rather than having to worry about concerts and host families and other people outside our little family.

That night, we made it to Kingman, AZ along historic Route 66. There had been some famous people that stayed at our motel so the rooms were all named after long forgotten country and western one-hit-wonders and amateur boxers who had once passed through. My journal tells me that the waitress was hitting on me that night but I can't seem to remember much about it. We were only 100 miles away from Las Vegas that night but Marci wouldn't let us leave the kids sleeping and drive 100 miles into the desert and come back in the same evening. In hindsight, she was probably right!

Next day (our sixth since leaving the San Antonio area) we finally reached our destination: Simi Valley, CA. We used to listen to California by Phantom Planet all the time on the van. When we were crossing the state line, we cranked the radio up all the way and sang along. Unfortunately, I misjudged it on my van and the song had finished before we reached the New Mexico/California border so we had to start the song over again.

We had been making great progress across the country from Texas – the speed limit had been 70mph since shortly after leaving San Antonio. When we hit California, the speed limit dropped to 55mph for vehicles with trailers which added a good two hours to our journey time.

By the time we hit Simi Valley, the children were starting to go crackers from cabin fever. We all stayed together for a few days in one host family in one of the most giant houses I've ever seen – they even had their own movie theatre. As a side note, it was at this host family that I finished my first book, a collection of stories for the children that we traveled with.[1] That night, joy of joys, after a two year wait Adam and I made it once more to In 'n' Out Burgers – easily the best burger chain in the Western hemisphere.

Brian McKinney (of Children's Hunger Fund) heads up our operation in California and he was the first to welcome us off the vans when we arrived in Simi. As I've said before, he is one of the wisest people I know and a joy to work with. I also need to mention by name Wendy from Cornerstone for all the work she did on getting us host families and Shayna for all the concert bookings she did. Wendy and Shayna we salute you! There was a group of other people who helped us in the background and although I can't

---

[1] Available at http://www.babymosquito.com
Sorry for the blatant cross marketing!

mention them all by name, we couldn't have done our tour without them.

Cornerstone was our 'home' church while we were in California. Just like Wayside, CBC and Maranatha in San Antonio, it seemed like we were at Cornerstone every few days. Pastor Chan has been to Uganda several times and continues to work closely with Pastor Peter, including broadcasting on Christian radio in Uganda.

The Church at Rocky Peak was just along the highway from Cornerstone and was where we did our first outdoor concert. It is also the only place I got yelled at for playing my music too loud. In my defense, it was before any of the audience was there – these two old ladies just happened to be walking through while I had my music on. To be fair, it was really, really loud but it was the Counting Crows – I mean, you can't really listen to them quietly, can you?

I had some amazing host families in Simi Valley – the Gerlachs, the Van Der Walls, the Johnsons, the Pratts, the Martins. It helped that most of them had swimming pools but they went so far above and beyond the call of duty and they continue to support Adam in his ministry in Uganda both in prayer and financially. I know that the other staff and kids had similar experiences with their host families and there is not space to name them all. The especially good thing about the Gerlachs and the Van Der Walls was the In 'n' Out Burgers right around the corner!

When we were in California, we took two of the most incredible drives I have ever been on. Lake Arrowhead is in the mountains above Los Angeles and we drove up the Top of the World Highway to sings at the Calvary Chapel up there. In my journal, I wrote that it was one of the most beautiful drives I had ever been on. The road twists and turns up through the mountain, past some beautiful scenery. It was incredible. When we arrived, members of the church were standing waiting for us with a huge 'Welcome Mwangaza' banner. We really ministered to people at that concert, took a huge offering, sponsored a load of kids and even ended up getting a few extra concerts arranged off the back of it including Reality Church in Carpinteria (more later). If it was up to me, we would only sing in Calvary Chapels – they are always so welcoming and really work hard to make sure we have a good time there.

A few days later, I had to revise my journal because we took a more beautiful drive than the one up to Lake Arrowhead. We had to drive way out into the desert to get to Palm Springs and even the children couldn't believe how hot it was. I was getting them all to put their hands on the roof and the windows inside the van to feel the heat coming in. Thank God for air conditioning! As we rounded a corner, we started the long drive through the most enormous wind farm. There were literally thousands and thousands of windmills all producing electricity. It was honestly one of the most amazing things I've ever seen. To my eyes, I have never seen anything man made quite so beautiful. It went on for miles and miles – wind turbines lined up in perfect rows. I would have loved to stop and take some photographs but the kids weren't too keen to get out of the van what with it being the middle of the desert.

Reality Church in Carpinteria was a proper skater's church. They meet in a big warehouse. Half of it has the seats for church and the other half has an indoor skate park. That's where Adam and I got into skateboarding, much to Marci's dismay – especially when she caught Corey on our skateboards. The church even gave Adam a skateboard.

It's nothing to do with tour but I have to tell you about one of the weirdest (and possibly most disgusting) things I have ever seen. I have a friend who lives in Atascadero which is further up the Pacific Coast Highway so while we were in Carpinteria, I went to visit her. We went to this car show in San Luis Obispo which was really cool – they had all these really neat '57 Chevys. But the main tourist draw of San Luis Obispo is called bubblegum alley. It's an alleyway where people stick their bubblegum on the wall. Apparently, people come from all over the world to see this. The walls on both sides are covered in many years worth of bubblegum. Some people have even used their bubblegum to make patterns and spell out words. So I used my bubblegum to stick a wrapper to the wall and wrote on it, 'Mark from Ireland was here, August, 2005.'

Our last concert in California was at The Father's House in Vacaville, CA. Sadly, this brings us to the end of my tour. I had to leave early to return to England to begin teacher training so in the next chapter, Adam will take up the story from the day we finally got a bus (the day after I left!). Fear not though, for my story is not over and I shall return but one chapter hence.

Leaving is never easy. Leaving early is twice as hard. The kids got me up on stage and sang to me at the last concert. Then they all attacked me with silly string in the parking lot! There were all kinds of tears the night before I left – although I had explained to them from day one that I would be leaving, some of them were just not old enough to understand why I had to go. Before I left, we took a group of the kids to Cold Stone Creamery so at least we could cry together over ice cream.

For me, I pray that my story with Mwangaza doesn't end here – I hope that my ministry with Mwangaza and these children will be ongoing. I continue to pray for them – that they will grow to be the great men and women of God that He desires. For them, the story of their tour is not yet over – one more month of tour remains, including some of the most grueling travel and concerts...

On The Road
Mark McKnight & Adam Ansel

Chapter 12

On The Bus

In early September we had the daunting task of traveling from the San Francisco area to various points in Oregon, out to Salt Lake City, Utah, and then back to Los Angeles via Las Vegas, Nevada, all in a three week period. Driving the vans that far and doing the number of concerts on the schedule was not an appealing thought so it was with enormous hearts of gratitude that we received the wonderful gift of a bus.

It was a big bus, top of the line and very modern, I don't really know any other way to describe it, but it has televisions, a bathroom, more seats than we could fill, and the coolest driver, a man we called Uncle Dave. He was in his sixties and has a great moustache, which makes anyone cool in my book.

The transition from three vans with two trailers to one bus took the greater part of one evening and the next morning. It wasn't until we unloaded everything out of the vans that we realized how much stuff we actually had. Of course we had the normal things like the sound equipment and product for selling, but we found old clothes, old food and even stuff that no one had ever seen before [side note: most of this stuff was probably accumulated and promptly forgotten about by Mark!]. Once we got everything unloaded into the parking lot of the church we separated things into two piles, what went above into the top of the bus and what went below. Underneath we put the sound equipment, all of the product, most of the bins of clothes, the big things really, and up top went the host family bags, sleeping bags, stuff that was accessed fairly regularly and things that we could use during bus rides.

Our first bus ride was a long one which took us from San Francisco to Bend, Oregon a drive which took about twelve hours including lunch, a few minutes to run around and stretch our legs and quite a number of bathroom breaks because although there was a toilet on the bus we didn't want twenty-some people using it.

That first ride was a lot of fun for the children because they all actually got to ride together instead of splitting up into different vehicles. They ate chicken for lunch and spent most of the ride shouting at each other from across the aisles and listening to music. We watched the movie 'Spy Kids' too which the children thoroughly enjoyed because there surely weren't movies in the vans. The first few rides there were no particular seating arrangements although the kids normally sat in the same area, but when we arrived in Sisters, OR, an official seating chart was made. Of course the kids grumbled at first, "I want to sit next to this one," and, "I want to sit in the back," were common complaints, but they soon came to be content with their seats.

We spent a lot of time on the bus during those three weeks because of the long distances between concert locations. It ate into a lot of time which normally would have been used for school so we took advantage of the long rides and the children revised on the bus. It was too noisy and unsteady to have someone teaching them so they were given work to do, which they did at their own pace, some of the younger ones following a very slow pace indeed. There was time for fun as well: on the really long trips we always watched a movie and the kids had free time to listen to music, talk, and sleep. We tried to do devotions on each trip – spending some time in praise and worship and then some time praying as well.

The trips were never boring even if they were really long, something interesting was always passing by outside the window and we stopped every few hours to use the bathroom and stretch our legs.

The last few weeks of tour were absolutely chaotic with, the numbers may not be exact, something like 18 concerts in 19 days, traveling from Portland, Oregon, to Salt Lake City, Utah and then back to Los Angeles, California. We were always tired needless to say, so the bus was a great refuge to retreat to. When we drove the vans, there wasn't as much room for stretching out and for those of who had to drive, there was no rest at all, so the greatest thing about the bus was the chance to sit back, relax, and truly enjoy the ride.

And that is where the story of tour must come to an end. The last two weeks of tour are a very intimate time when we say our goodbyes and go our separate ways, moments that I feel are better left unspoken.

However, there are still some moments on tour and some loose ends that must still but have not yet been fully laid bare.

On The Road
Mark McKnight & Adam Ansel

Chapter 13

GMA Dove Awards

Pastor Peter has been involved for some years now with something of a research project with Compassion International. Compassion is a wonderful organization that does some incredible work throughout the world. In Gaba, we have many children sponsored through Compassion who meet on a regular basis for bible studies. There is also the Early Childhood Project which something akin to a pre-school. We have children from 0-3 years that attend and I'm not joking when I say they are some of the cutest kids in Gaba: they really love to have their pictures taken.

Peter is a close friend of Compassion's country director and as a result, we often have visitors to Gaba to see what kind of things Compassion is doing on the ground. One of our visitors was Nicole C. Mullen who, when she was at church in Gaba, heard Mwangaza performing. If you haven't heard of Nicole C. Mullen, go out and buy her CD. She's become a huge supporter of the choir and she sings some great songs of her own. When Nicole was in Gaba, she decided that she wanted to perform with these children when they came to America. At that stage, we didn't have any visas or even any bookings so we weren't sure if we were yet going to America.

However, God had his plans already set in stone and it wasn't long before Nicole was invited to sing at the Gospel Music Association's Dove Awards in Nashville, TN. She had the idea that she would like to perform with Mwangaza for this concert. The

Dove Awards are like a Christian version of the Grammies. It's the one night that almost everyone in the Christian music world turns out in their finery to celebrate not in their own accomplishments but in what God is doing in the field of Christian music. I remember the meeting when Tom told us that we had been invited to go. As an organization of integrity, we were committed to the bookings we had made – we weren't going to cancel a booking just because a better opportunity had come along. Tom explained what going to Nashville would mean – 3 concerts at Baylor University on the Monday, drive through the night to Nashville, three sound checks and two concerts on the Tuesday, one more sound check and the dove awards on the Wednesday and then drive through the night back to Dallas for a couple of hard earned days off. It was a unanimous vote to go – we knew it would be hard but it would have been crazy to turn down such an incredible opportunity.

Did I mention this was an incredible opportunity? I can honestly say that never in my life have I been so blown away by God's grace. Not his mercy, but his grace. Mercy is when we don't get what we deserve to get. Grace is when we get something that we don't deserve. This was another one of God's kicks in the pants for me – remember like the one in the airport where he told me that I should have believed right from the very start. Well, you'd think I would have learned my lesson! But there was always that little voice of doubt in the back of my mind saying, 'It's just luck that you're here. Everything could go all wrong. The organization might lose money from this tour. This whole project might fail.' You see, somehow I had missed God's memo that his hand would be on the tour. I think everyone else on the tour knew except me. Like I said – I'm more of a Peter than a Philip. So when we went to Nashville, I wasn't even expecting a fraction of one percent of what God had in store for us.

One lazy afternoon in Gaba, while the kids were talking, Adam and I were talking about the program that the choir would perform. The choir was practicing 'Above All' – that song that Lenny LeBlanc wrote but that Michael W. Smith sings. Adam told me that he didn't really like the songs or at least it didn't really fit in with the rest of the program. In fact, his actual words were, "The only good thing that can come from Mwangaza singing that song is that Michael W. Smith might hear it and want to sing it with us." Read on and I'll explain why I'm telling you this story.

Every year, on the night before the Dove Awards ceremony, Compassion has a banquet for all of its supporters in the Christian music industry. Since it was Compassion who had footed most of the bill to get us there, they asked us to sing a couple of songs at their dinner. A few years ago, I applied to work with Compassion as an Artist Relations Manager (which was just a fancy title for liaising with the artists and bands who helped to promote Compassion) so I knew that there would be some fairly important players from the Christian music industry at the banquet. I never put two and two together, however. Early in the day, we had sound checked for the Dove Awards ceremony and while the children were on stage, a call came through saying that Michael W. Smith was also performing at the banquet and would we be interested in singing with him? Err...YES!!! I mean, ask a stupid question, right? He had suggested a song that we didn't know so we were left with the choice of rushing out, buying a CD, learning the song and then teaching it to the kids or telling Michael W. Smith what we wanted to sing. So we took the rude option and told his people that we didn't know the song and could we sing Above All instead.

Our kids sang a few of their own songs before dinner and then we all sat down to a wonderful three course meal. It was the funniest thing – proper posh food. The kids hadn't a clue what they were eating. In fact, mostly they were scared to touch it because they didn't recognize a thing on their plates. After the meal, there were a few speeches and presentations and then Michael W. Smith got up on stage to sing some of his songs. At the very end, he invited our children back to the stage to sing with him and together they sang Above All. I had positioned myself to take some video footage of the occasion but it was only half way through the song that I remembered what Adam had said two months before. My journal entry for the occasion is gloriously understated:

> "About two months ago, Adam said that the only good thing that could possibly come from singing Above All is that Michael W. Smith might hear it and want to sing it with us. Well, we've just sang it with him."

I almost fell over when I remembered it, and I couldn't keep the video camera still for laughing. I'm sure the people behind me were wondering what had come over me – maybe they thought I had caught the Spirit or something! And then I heard God's tiny whisper in my ear, "I told you so."

At that point I finally accepted that we were right in the middle of God's will and instead of being amazed at God's blessings on this choir, I began to look for and expect them. That was just as well because of the things that were going to happen within the next couple of days.

Let me skip forward a couple of weeks, back in San Antonio, to finish our Michael W. Smith story. At the time, Michael was in the middle of recording his most recent album. One of his songs for the album was about the ravage of HIV/AIDS across the world but particularly on the continent of Africa. He and his producer had this great idea that they would fly to San Antonio to record some vocals with the kids for his album. After all that had already passed, I had ceased to be surprised by this kind of thing.

We had booked the studio out for the whole afternoon but we were finished in half the time we had booked which is a tribute to the professionalism of our children. I can honestly say without reservation that Michael W. Smith is one of the nicest people I have ever met – he was a joy to record with and I know the rest of our staff and children feel the same. I can only hope that we have blessed him as much with our ministry as he has blessed us as a choir and us as the worldwide family of God with his ministry.

Michael's entire family was there – wife and kids. They were going on vacation as soon as they left the studio but instead of leaving and trying to catch an earlier flight, when we had finished recording, Michael picked up Marius' old guitar and right there in the live room of the studio, we began to worship. We worshipped the living God there in the studio as a family in the body of Christ with representatives from three continents. There's some wonderful video footage of our worship which we hope to release as a bonus feature on a DVD some time soon.

If you will allow me a little personal vanity, as we were leaving the studio, Michael spotted my accent and was talking to me about Ireland. His actual words were, "Ireland is the most beautiful country I have ever been to." Of course, I already know Ireland is the most beautiful country but it's always nice to see someone else appreciating it!

I'm also hearing whispers that we might be doing some work with him in the upcoming tour (2006) but that's just a rumor at the moment so I won't tell anyone if you don't – it's just for prayer, you understand.

Let's go back to the Dove Awards because aside from the Compassion banquet, God had much more in store with us. As soon as I got back to the hotel room, I called Adam who was still in Uganda and related what had just happened. His response, "I'M A PROPHET!"

On the day of the Dove Awards, we arrived at 10:00am and were literally stuck in our dressing room all day long. The kids were going out of their heads with cabin fever so we were taking turns to go into the auditorium to watch people doing their sound checks. While we were in there, CeCe Winans was doing her sound check. Now, you need to understand that more or less the only two

CDs we ever listened to on our van were CeCe Winans and Kirk Franklin. So as I looked at the backstage pass around my neck, I thought, 'let me see if CeCe Winans has time to come and talk to the kids.' I set off into the labyrinth of corridors to find her once she had finished sound check and when I found her, she was surrounded by her entourage. It was clear that she really didn't have time to come to see the kids but she was very gracious about it – maybe some day she will have the privilege of meeting our kids.

Next up on stage to sound check was Kirk Franklin. Now if the kids liked CeCe Winans, they LOVED Kirk Franklin. They know all the words to all his songs and they regularly start singing them for no reason at all. CeCe had been surrounded by dancers, minders and goodness knows who else but Kirk was just wandering around the corridors by himself. I introduced myself and asked if he had time to come to meet the children. The kids went absolutely crazy when he walked through the door. It was the biggest smile I have ever seen on Nicolas' face. Actually, most of the kids recognized Kirk when he came in the room. All of them except Daphine – she had been listening to her CD player when I had told everyone who was about to visit with them. When he came into the dressing room, she took off her headphones and in her sweetest voice, with Kirk standing behind me, said, "Uncle, who is that?"

It was such a special moment – our kids sang one of their songs for Kirk and he even invited us to his house in Dallas for a pool party. Unfortunately, our schedules didn't work out and we were never able to hook up. It was just as the kids were singing for Kirk that my friend Jeff arrived in the room after having blagged his way into the building. I will tell you Jeff's story in a moment – it's not really related to Mwangaza but I want to give God the glory because Jeff's blessings that came from us being in Nashville really do just that.

Nicole C. Mullen, as I said before has been one of our biggest fans. She too came to San Antonio to record with us – our song is on her latest album and it sounds great. It was because of her visit to Gaba that we ended up going to Nashville so it was a joy to see her and her team at the Dove Awards. We spent most of the day with Nicole and her dancers in the dressing room teaching each other to dance – Nicole taught our kids how to dance American and our kids taught Nicole and her dancers how to dance African. Nicole brought her family to hang out with us during the day. In fact I think some of our boys developed a bit of a crush on Nicole's daughter but that is another story.

After I phoned Adam to tell him what had happened the next person I phoned was Pete because he was one of the few other people who I knew would appreciate what had just happened. Pete said, "Wait a minute. Where are you?" When I told him we were in Nashville, he told me that one of our best friends, Jeff, was in Nashville for the G.M.A. Conference that goes on every year before the Dove Award. So I got straight on the phone with Jeff and invited him to hang out with us at the Dove Awards. He wasn't expecting to hear from me so when I phoned up and offered him backstage passes he didn't believe me at first. Our conversation went something like this.

"Jeff, what are you doing tomorrow night?"
"Not much."
"Are you going to the Dove Awards?"
"No."
"Do you want to go to the Dove Awards?"
"Of course, but despite the fact that tickets are sold out, they start at $200 so I think they are a little out of my price range."
"Do you want me to get you in?"
"Of course."
"Do you want me to get you backstage passes?"
Sound of Jeff picking phone up off the floor.

Jeff is a festival organizer in Ireland.[2] He just started a couple of years ago so it's all still in its infancy but Jeff has big visions. He's been through the fire big time but I know God's just getting ready to bless his little Irish socks off. Pray for him though. Right now. Just say, 'Please God, look after Jeff, Amen.' There, wasn't that easy?

I'm sidetracking here a bit but since this book is all about lifting up the name of Jesus, you need to hear this story and I know Jeff won't mind me telling it. We all used to work on this festival called Summer Madness. Jeff, Pete and I and almost all my best friends back in Ireland. It still runs every year at the start of the summer but we've all moved on to bigger and better things. One year, this girl showed up at the festival called Steff. Steff was into black magic, the occult and the whole nine yards. Actually, what she didn't know was that the devil had her right where he wanted her, or so he thought. The outdoor festival's main stage was in a circus big top and Satan had sent Steff to Madness to burn down the big top. Plain and simple – she told us the story herself. But you know, God had other plans. Two words for you – already defeated. Devil didn't think Steff would fail him but God stepped in, changed her life around and turned Steff into the most on fire Christian I have seen in my life bar none. Admittedly, the girl was absolutely bonkers – the first time I met her was when we went to see the

---

[2] http://www.tarafestival.com

Rocky Horror Show. If Jesus said, "I have come that you might have life in all its fullness," then Steff lived life in all its fullness — she couldn't stop talking about what Jesus was doing in her life. Her heart was opened up to the needs of the world. And only God can take the glory.

The reason I'm reminded of Steff is that she dated Jeff for a few brief weeks. In the fullness of time we'll understand why one sleepy Sunday afternoon on a highway about 4 miles from where I grew up, God chose to call Steff home. Steff's car went under an eighteen-wheeler and she was killed instantly. Her funeral was one of the biggest her church has seen. Steff's brief ministry of a few short years blessed literally hundreds, maybe thousands, of people. And then Jesus welcomed Steff with open arms into his kingdom. I'm no preacher but even I can see the amazing grace at work in Steff's life. There's hope for me yet.

> Amazing Grace, how sweet the sound
> That saved a wretch like me
> I once was lost but now am found
> Was blind, but now I see.

Read Steff's story again. Makes you think, doesn't it? There are hundreds of hearts in Northern Ireland that cry a private tear, including mine and Jeff's, every time we think about Steff. I wish that our kids had the chance to meet Steff.

As I said, I know I've digressed but I've just heard that still small voice of calm (I'm getting better at hearing it now) which said I should include Steff's story here.

Anyway, Jeff runs a Christian music festival in Ireland. It's in the very same field where I met him all those years ago. I know it was God that ordained our meeting in Nashville — Jeff came and hung out backstage at the awards with us and spent most of his time talking to Toby Mac, Rebecca St. James, Steven Curtis Chapman...you get the idea. Jeff got talking to some guy about Tara Festival. He had no idea who the guy was — they were just talking. The guy asked him if he could have one artist at the festival, who would it be? So Jeff replied, "Well, I don't know — I mean, it's not like I'm going to get Amy Grant!" as a bit of a joke. The guy's reply? "Actually, I'm Amy Grant's lawyer. Here's my card — call me on Monday morning and we'll see what we can work out."

God truly does work in mysterious ways.

As soon as the Dove Awards ceremony was finished, we had to get straight back onto our bus to come back to Dallas. We were all so blown away by everything that happened, it took us a couple of weeks to process it all but even now I am amazed by how God blessed us that weekend. And all glory must go to him because there is nothing that we could have done to get us there. I often wonder if, even with unlimited resources, we could have done everything the same in our own strength and every time, the answer is a resounding no. Some people would pay good money to do what we did that weekend in their whole lifetime. God opened the doors and blessed us more that we could ever have imagined.

Chapter 14

MINISTRY

A big part of what we do on tour (possibly the biggest part) is ministry. Mwangaza is not about raising money for building schools and orphanages in Africa. That just happens to be a fortuitous by product. Much more important, and the focus of Mwangaza right from the very start, even before they came on tour, has been the ministry. The ministry of Mwangaza as a choir and the children as individuals has and continues to be incredible. There have been times when I have stood back, amazed at how our children have ministered to people.

It's difficult for me to tell you all the stories of how these children ministered because it was in so many different places at different times and in different ways.

At many of our concerts, the pastor of the church had an altar call where he invited people to give their lives to Jesus. There was rarely any preaching – God drew people to himself just by the ministry of Mwangaza's singing and dancing. I don't know if anybody kept official figures but there are now a bunch of people all across America who are now in the Kingdom because of Mwangaza's ministry.

Before our concert, the children and as many staff as are available do devotions and pray for the souls of the people who will listen to them. Often, the technical teams joined in with these devotions using 2-way radios – usually we were too busy preparing for the concert to be present but oftentimes the children would pray for us over the airwaves using the radio that Lillian carried during the concert. The pastor of the church was always invited to participate in our devotions and many times he asked Lillian to forget about part of the concert and lead the audience in worship to let them experience something of the faith of these children.

The children didn't just minister collectively as a choir but also as individuals. I remember one time we were staying with a host family and we happened to meet their neighbor in the street.

After the neighbor had departed, the host family mentioned that he was not saved. Without any prompting, our boys had a huddle and decided that they wanted to go to the neighbor's house to witness to him. When we went to talk to him, all the memory verses that the boys had learned clicked into place and they were able to explain their faith to the man in their own way. The man listened carefully and although he didn't make any commitment that night, who knows what seeds our boys may have planted?

Coming from outside the American culture, the children were constantly asking questions about things they didn't understand – why do Americans do this or that? What does such and such a thing mean? We stayed with regular people and so saw them at their worst and best: families fighting with one another, children with a bad attitude towards their parents, parents who have all but given up hope on their own children. I remember one family we stayed with who had two boys who just watched TV or played their computer games in every spare minute, despite all kinds of toys around their house. Needless to say, when we arrived there were all kinds of tantrums because they weren't allowed to switch on the television. We stayed with the same family for four days and our boys had a big influence on those two boys.

We bumped into the family a few concerts later and they said that after they had dropped us off, their boys had come home and one had started playing with their dog and the other got his action figures out. When mom asked why they weren't watching TV, they said that they didn't really want to – they would much rather play with some real toys. It doesn't sound like much but if you're a parent, you'll know what a big deal this really is.

Occasionally, we have entered a house where there is no spirit of peace – always people shouting at one another and two days later when we depart, it is like a different house – the example and ministry of our children was incredible as people saw the love of Jesus through them and saw something of how they need to love one another.

I know that James and Lillian in particular as a married couple were able to minister to many of their host families – James used to arrive every morning and tell us stories about how he had been praying with and for his host families and ministering to them.

I can only hope and pray that my own ministry as a chaperone for Mwangaza has been as exemplary as that of the rest of the staff and children.

Chapter 15

FUNDRAISING

As I mentioned in the last chapter, although fundraising was something we did on the tour, it was not the sole intent – mostly, we were there to minister. Fundraising was a by product that has and will continue to bless the community in Gaba and the wider community of believers in Africa.

I can honestly say, hand on heart, that I have no idea how we did financially out of the tour. However, I can remember every person who put up their hand to say that they accepted Jesus and at the end of the day that is what matters. Even if we lost a fortune on plane tickets, sound equipment and miscellaneous expenses, if one person accepted Jesus as their Savior then it was all worthwhile.

That is not to say that we did lose a fortune. I know that we must have at least broken even – otherwise I would have known about it. I also know that with the outpouring of love, generosity and kindness we received in every way, we must have done all right.

Let me put it this way. The first time I went to Bethany Village, we had to stop at the public dock because didn't have a dock on our own land. We had to ride through progressively worse jungle on the back of motorcycle taxis to get to our land. There were a bunch of squatters living on the land. Pastor Peter conducted our tour through the different bits of land that we owned and we climbed the hill to look out over the lake. The land was empty – mostly untilled bush or scrubland with squatters trying to scratch out a living farming a small plot or by fishing.

Pastor Peter's model is to build something that will last. If the funding disappears tomorrow, at least the schools will still be there. The children's homes will still be standing. The clinics, churches and all of the other projects will still be there even if the money disappears. But the point is that they are there and that is largely attributable to the money raised on the Mwangaza tour.

So please, celebrate the achievements of the Mwangaza Children's Choir: the schools, children's homes, clinics, churches, workshops and women's projects. But celebrate more the lives that have been saved through the ministry in America and in Africa. Let me complicate things a little more though. Through the projects that have been financed by 'Mwangaza money,' many more people in Uganda have come and are coming to know Jesus as we reach out to the community providing for their physical, emotional and most of all spiritual needs.

Chapter 16

We Also Have Fun Days!

Tour life is hectic, but at least occasionally we take some time to relax, blow off some steam and just have a good time. Birthday parties, staff nights-out, play time and special days are always an important part of tour – since these kids work so hard to minister to everyone they come into contact with, the least we can do is make sure they have a great time on their days off. Admittedly, planning for the kids to have fun can be a big headache in itself for the staff but that's a fairly small price to pay.

I've already told you some of the stories before but let me write a whole chapter about some of the most fun things that happened to us on tour and maybe some of the funny stories that go along with them.

For some reason, and unlike any other tour I have been on, swimming was a major part of our tour. A huge number of our host families had their own pool or at least took us over to a neighbor's house to swim there. To us, swimming seems a little dull and boring but I can tell you that our kids got the greatest thrill out of swimming on tour.

In Gaba, the only people who swim in swimming pools are the rich people. I don't know of any swimming pools on our side of the city – they are usually just in the swanky hotels. If you want to swim, the only thing you can do is to risk swimming in the lake and then you have a variety of options: dysentery (fever, vomiting, abdominal cramps), bilharzia (a parasite that can mess with all kinds of things) and a variety of other waterborne illnesses are all available.

Swimming on tour was something else completely. I've mentioned before how much Dwayne loved to swim. He seemed to be in the pool constantly. As the dutiful uncle, I was usually in the pool swimming with him. It took me a long time to work something out thoug: Adam and I were constantly eating fast food on tour, particularly when we got to California. After all, who can resist In 'n' Out Burgers? But I couldn't work out why even though I was eating so many hamburgers I wasn't really putting on any weight. Then one day it occurred to me: in an average week, I was probably spending up to ten hours in the water in various host family swimming pools. If you were a host family and you had a pool, at least you have contributed to my non-obesity!

The first host family we went to that had a pool was in Texas in the middle of March. Those who live in San Antonio will know that this is no time to be venturing into an unheated outdoor pool but nothing would satisfy the boys until I let them go swimming. So we all quickly got changed and went outside to jump in the pool. Since the boys hadn't really swum much before, they were a little hesitant to jump straight in. So I explained that I would count to three and we would all jump in together. Martin, Ponsiano and I lined up at the edge of the pool and I began to count. When I got to three, Martin and I both pretended to jump but then stopped before we left the poolside. Ponsiano, however, jumped straight in. What he hadn't thought of was that he didn't really know how to swim so I had to jump in straight after him to rescue him.

With all joking aside, teaching these children how to swim was one of the joys of being on tour. In retrospect, it seems like a microcosm of the spiritual growth I see in them every time I return to Uganda. At the start of the tour, there were a few children who flatly refused to even venture into the water. But with time and patience, even the most timid swimmers were jumping into the water, diving, swimming and playing all kinds of games. The two Dorothys and Gladys were my lengthiest project. I tried and tried and tried to reassure them but they were always so nervous. Eventually, Dorothy N became the best diver in the whole choir!

By the end of tour, things got a bit lonely for me in the swimming pool – I had taught everybody to swim so well that they all went off to play their own games and left me to swim by myself. They just didn't need me any more. Isn't that a great analogy though – that we've helped these children become self sufficient. They have grown up enough to not just do something with our help but to do things by themselves.

Not wanting to sound like I've been sucked in by the corporate schmooze, how could we bring these children to America without experiencing the pinnacle of American entertainment: the theme park in general and Disneyland in particular?

Let us start with the 'lesser' theme parks and hopefully come to Walt's wonderland as our climax. While we were still in San Antonio, some of the kids visited Fiesta Texas (Six Flags) with host families and then the whole choir went to Sea World.

On the night that our boys went to Fiesta Texas, there happened to be another couple of other host families there with their kids. So we all spent the evening riding the dodgem cars and going on rides until we were sick! Actually, that night I was almost sick – must have been something I ate, so early on I decided to let the boys go on the rides and I would watch.

Ponsiano and Nicolas were funny that night. I really wanted to get some pictures of our kids on the Carousel so I explained to them that about a hundred years ago, it would have been the only ride at the fair and I wanted to get some photographs. I managed to convince them to go on it. Unfortunately, I didn't manage to convince them to enjoy it. I think they just didn't get it – they wanted the fast roller coasters so I have photos of the two boys going around on the Carousel looking absolutely miserable.

Fiesta Texas (like most theme parks) has a big fireworks display and laser show at the end of the night. Texans are very patriotic and this was reflected in the content of the show. It was interesting to hear some of the questions about why Americans were so patriotic and I suggested that they should ask their host families (since I'm not American myself!). It let the host families think about the reasons for their own patriotism and it let our kids think about patriotism for their own country. I'm no politician but I'm all for properly placed patriotism, regardless of your country.

While we were at Fiesta Texas, the funniest thing happened. Auntie Sarah was wearing one of those hair pieces that make it look like you have braids in. While she was upside down on the roller coaster, it fell off and she never saw it again. The kids thought it was hilarious.

Sea World, San Antonio was a whole different experience. We all went together one day as a proper 'tour day off.' We arrived first thing in the morning and discussed what we would do. We decided that Adam, JD, and I would look after the boys and everyone else would stay with the girls. So we set off and did what all boys do – went to look for the roller coasters. I was fit as a fiddle that day and there was hardly anyone in the park so we spent all morning going on the roller coasters and water rides. Apart from one coaster in England, they are easily the best roller coasters I have ever been on.

Soon, lunch time rolled around and we met up with the girls and the rest of the staff. We told them about all the rides we had been on and the girls told us all about the shows they had seen. When it came to discussing the afternoon, James and Lillian decided that they wanted to see some more shows and would it be okay if we took the girls on the rides for the afternoon. So Adam, JD and I spent all afternoon on the roller coasters too.

We all went to see Shamu (the killer whale) together and of course we sat in the splash zone so that we would get soaked.

Kemah Boardwalk outside Houston was one of my best days on tour. We didn't get there until late afternoon – the sun was starting to drop in the sky so it wasn't too hot. There was hardly anybody there and we were able to walk straight on to most of the rides that we wanted.

Daphine was the smallest person in the choir and was a little overawed by all the rides so she started going on the kiddie rides and made me stay with her. It wasn't long before she got bored and she made me go on the proper rides with her. By the time we left, she had been on all of the big rides and had even gone on some that other kids were reluctant to go on.

It was at Kemah Boardwalk that we went on the pirate ship with some of the girls – the one that swings back and forth. It had taken us a good half hour to persuade some of the girls to go on with us. That was the ride that Dorothy A cried the whole way through and when it was finished she immediately asked us if we could go again.

One of the rides even broke while we were there and we waited suspended in the air for a good five minutes before an engineer came and pressed the right button to let us back down to ground level again. I was a bit worried that it might knock some of the children's confidence in the rides but they were having too much fun – they immediately joined the line for a different ride.

The climax of our theme park experience was our visit to Disneyland. We all stayed together the night before and drove to the park early in the morning. Fred Martin from Children's Hunger Fund acted as our guide for the day – he worked there as a teenager so he was an able tour guide.

It was interesting seeing the reaction from the children to Disneyland. Unlike most children in the west, they have not grown up with constant exposure to the Disney franchise and as a result, often didn't quite know who some of the characters were or the relevance of some of the scenery.

Despite all this, Disneyland was a wonderful day out. For part of the time we had a reporter and a photographer from the Orange County Register with us, so we had to be on our best behavior. Disneyland is exhausting, especially going to the vans to bring back the lunch and then the dinner too.

For weeks, we had been building up the Indiana Jones ride – telling the kids how good it was and promising who we would sit beside. Finally, the moment had come. We spent ages in the line waiting for our turn and finally we got into the jeeps and started our journey. Unfortunately, the ride was a little bit too good. A bunch of our kids came off the ride with tears streaming. I thought some of the girls might never speak to me again for making them go through it. Years ago, the first time I went on that ride, one of the girls I was with spent the whole ride hiding beneath the dashboard of the jeep because she didn't want to watch any of it.

Although swimming and theme parks were fun, they weren't the only fun things that we did on tour. For conservation of time and space I won't write about all of these things but to give you a taster of what kinds of things we got up to, here are a few things that we've done in our down time…

Every couple of months, we would take a few days out and go for a camp – swimming, playing games, dancing, drawing pictures, doing devotions and relaxing away from the very public life that we lead. We can really let our hair down and be ourselves. Usually, we let the kids decide what they want to do as it is their camp. Of course, that usually means that we staff have to work harder at camp than we do normally.

We also went to see basketball, baseball, football and hockey games. We went snowboarding, skateboarding, fishing, four wheeling and bowling. We flew in planes and hot air balloons, boated on lakes, floated down rivers in an inner tube and surfed in the ocean. We drove in Mustangs, Hummers, fire engines and police cars. We saw the space shuttle, the Hollywood sign, the Grand Canyon and the strip in Las Vegas. We went to countless zoos, parks, swimming pools and all you can eat buffets. We were in a parade, we flew kites, we cheered for high school basketball teams, we ate until we were pogged to the eyeballs and we created a Pepsi shortage in southern California!

James got married, Lillian got pregnant, Sarah lost her hair piece (see above), Joshua got healed, Marci was a star, Tana turned sixteen, JD got arrested (by his host family who was a cop), Adam fell into the Grand Canyon (I have the pictures to prove it), and I fell in and out of love.

So who says ministry is boring?

On The Road
Mark McKnight & Adam Ansel

Chapter 17

BACK HOME IN AFRICA

In Gaba, some things change literally overnight while others never seem to change. As I write, it is over a year since the kids left America to return to Uganda. All of us are a year older and a year wiser. James and Lillian have a baby daughter called Love Joy now. I'm an elementary school teacher in England. Adam is living and working full time in Gaba. Tana got her high school diploma and now she's ready to start college. Joshua is studying music and media in Uganda. Sarah is teaching the Sunday School in Gaba. Nobody has heard from JD for months – he may still be in prison since his host family arrested him!

Honestly, it breaks my heart that God called Adam to Uganda before me. I wake up every morning and ask God, 'can I go today?' but every morning He tells me to wait a little longer. I guess I just have to wait for God's perfect timing. Like I've said before – either I'm not ready for Africa or else Africa isn't ready for me.

Let me fill you in on the details. I finally made it back to Africa this past summer (2005). I had just compressed an entire degree into one year so I was physically and emotionally exhausted by the time I got there. I had all kinds of problems before I left – for a while, I didn't have a job to come back to. There was even a time when it looked like I wasn't going to be able to go to Africa at all. But I had learned some hard lessons the previous year (see above!) and wasn't going to forget them in a hurry. So I persisted and eventually made it to Gaba about 2 weeks later than planned.

Ironically, when I arrived Adam and his parents were on safari so I had to phone all my friends to find someone to pick me up at the airport. That drive into Gaba from the airport is always a blessing. There's a saying in Gaba that if children could vote, Adam and I would be mayor. So driving (or walking) through Gaba is always a social occasion.

I won't bore you with all the details of my own personal trip because let's face it, the only person who cares about that is me! But one year on and Mwangaza is still going strong. In fact, the whole church is going from strength to strength.

Let me start with the church. The empty land across the lake now has five children's homes, a school, a church, a campsite and a variety of other projects at various stages of completion. A sizeable proportion of this can be attributed to the Mwangaza tour – both directly and indirectly. Adam wrote a report on Bethany village which has been included as the next chapter. The church now has gone from three or four projects close to Gaba to fourteen projects all around the country and one or two further afield. The model of a church, a school, a clinic and a children's home is working. It provides not just for a community's spiritual needs but also its physical, emotional and educational needs. The Africa Renewal Ministries model is all about renewing the whole community every way it can.

The church in Gaba continues to grow. Business mentoring has become a large part of the men's ministry, including micro-financing for viable business propositions. The women's ministry has been given a big boost from all the craft sales during the Mwangaza tour. We now broadcast twice weekly across the country on Christian television and friends of the organization broadcast several times a week on Ugandan Christian radio.

Mwangaza past, present and future are thriving. Every time I see our kids they have grown further towards the great Christian men and women of God that I pray they will become.

Ponsiano really ministers to the church through his music – he drums in the band most Sunday mornings and it is always a joy to see him using the talents that God has given him. We spent a few days at camp with the lower high school kids. Ponsiano was practically one of the leaders, even though he should just have been there as a camper. I am certain that one day he will be an excellent pastor.

Every time I go to a Mwangaza practice, there's always a group of our girls there helping out, teaching the younger kids how to sing and telling them about tour – mentoring them. Kids like Angella N, Angella M and Joy.

Angella M has been almost at the top of her class consistently ever since she got home. She's still a goofball but she works so hard. Her sister, Joy, has been doing really well at school too.

Dwayne has finally started to grow. He's at boarding school and he loves it. When I first met Dwayne, he was a shy seven year old who didn't talk much. His clothes were always dirty because he spent so much time rolling in the dirt! Now he's a confident, articulate young man with things to say and opinions on what is happening. And (usually) his clothes are clean and he's smartly dressed. His mom helps run the internet café beside the church so we see him all the time. Usually, he'll ride with us in the car if we're going somewhere just to give him something to do.

Daphine is always around Gaba with her friends. We see her in the street every now and then and she goes to A.W.A.N.A. (children's activities) every Saturday afternoon. Since tour, she's really grown and matured. She too has become a confident young lady and I am sure that as she grows, she will become even more of a leader. She's been doing really well in school. We have a deal going that if she gets top marks at the end of this year I have to buy her a bicycle.

Some of the kids went to boarding schools around the city and, since we had a big car, we picked most of them up at the end of term. Dorothy A and Gladys were at the same school. Neither had an easy term but I'm glad they were there to keep one another company. Of everyone I know in the world, those two have the most beautiful spirits. The only person who even comes close is Dorothy's mom – a truly great woman who has triumphed over great adversities throughout her life and still has a smile on her face.

Martin's mom runs one of the children's homes that the church funds. We used to go and hang out there most evenings. Martin was off at boarding school but his sister was the only kid in a home of 72 that went to a different school up the hill so we walked her to school most mornings. When Martin got back from boarding school, he spent almost the whole vacation at our house, even sleeping on our sofa. I think he was a little jealous of the time we had been spending with his little sister!

Freedom is one of the kids who stays at the children's home. It's just round the corner from our house so he seems to be around all the time too. Dorothy N used to be at the home all the time too, although she didn't live there. I think she was there visiting friends. Dorothy's smile was always something that brought me great joy while we were on tour, partly because it was so rare. Now that she's home though, she's smiling all the time.

Every time she sees us in the street, there's always a smile and something to talk about. She's studying hard and is really maturing in her faith.

Unfortunately, there were some kids who I didn't manage to catch up with – the school holidays were at just the wrong time so I had to leave before some kids had finished their term. But the reports that I get are that everyone is doing well – their grades are up, they're trying hard and they haven't lost their vision of how they might help make their country and their continent a better place.

All our kids have been affected much more than they will probably ever realize through tour. They are confident, they have thought out what they want to do with their lives and most importantly, they all have a strong faith in Jesus. I have long been of the opinion that part of the reason we take the children on tour is to implant in their minds the idea that there is no reason that they can't have everything that people have in the West and more if they put their minds to it. That they can be instrumental in changing Africa.

In the concert, James used to ask some of the children what they might like to be when they grow up. Way back at the start of the tour, they didn't really know. However, as they toured and as we ministered to them, they began to realize ways that they could help their own country to be greater. By the end of the tour, they all had ideas fixed in their minds – teachers, doctors, engineers and best of all pastors. Leah wanted to be president. That always got a laugh in concerts but I used to tell her every day that there was no reason why she couldn't be president. Yes, she might have to work hard and of course it will be difficult but I pray that Leah will never waver in her dream. I wish I could write it in giant letters on her house, encourage her every day and stand beside her and sock anybody who sniggers or says that it will never happen.

I have this theory that if you only have small dreams, you will only ever accomplish small things. But if you have big dreams, huge dreams, the kind that seem impossible without God's help then you've got much better odds of doing something really great. That's what I love about Adam – he encourages me (and vice versa) to think big. Some of the ideas we come up with will never, ever happen. Actually, <u>most</u> of them will never happen period. But if just one of them were to happen, that would really be something. Between us, we have published two books with another eight or so in the pipeline. We've recorded four albums of our own material and worked on a variety of others. There's at least another three planned within the next two years. Adam has directed two movies, is working on another two and I have three in pre-production.

We've also shot a bunch of documentaries and edited all kinds of projects.

On tour, I pray every day that some of this will rub off on the kids. That they will realize that they are capable of accomplishing whatever their heart desires with God's help. Now that I see them back in Gaba, walking through their own streets with their own people, I can see the difference that we have made in their lives. Every one of them I know is going to do great things for the kingdom.

We try to minister to the kids in Gaba as much as we can – praying with them, playing with them and encouraging them. The truth of the matter, however, is that the Mwangaza children are the most effective children's pastors in the whole village. Almost without exception, their lives are exemplary – an example to their peers and even to most of the adults living in the village. I know that I can certainly learn plenty from their faith, their commitment, their confidence and their resolve to make Gaba, Uganda and Africa a better place.

If this book ministers in no other way, know that you have made such a difference in these few children's lives. Leave aside all the extra kids who have been sponsored as a result of the tour. Leave aside all the children who now have a roof over their heads, a proper school and quality healthcare. Just by inviting us into your homes, I promise you have made Africa a better place. Watch this space for I know you are going to see incredible things from Mwangaza children – past, present and future.

As I see it, one of the big problems in Africa is that people don't expect much out of life. They aren't content with their lot but they don't expect it to be any better. Many see no reason in working hard to improve their lot. It comes back to small dreams producing small results. Just by seeing how you live – your houses, cars, churches and your lives in general, these children have begun to expect something more out of life. They have decided that there could and should be more to life for them and their families. They have begun to expect God to do big things in their own lives and the lives of those around them. It's not any kind of narrow minded prosperity gospel. This is God's people holding firm to the promises that God has given them. Every day I hope someone reminds these kids what Jeremiah chapter 29 says:

> "For I know the plans I have for you," declares the Lord, "plans to prosper you and not to harm you, plans to give you hope and a future."

I don't believe that God will give me all the desires of my heart. I'd really love to be a world famous author. It'd be great to have a number one hit record or win Best Director at the Oscars or marry Beyoncé. What? It could happen! Actually, I really believe that with God's help it could happen (maybe not the marrying Beyoncé part) but that's not my point.

I also can't believe in a God who is intent on making me do the one thing that I really don't want to. He wants to prosper me – give me success in my ministry, fulfill some of the desires of my heart and accomplish great things through me.

So if you see Leah, tell her that with God's help, she can easily become the president.

Those same kids who arrived in America almost two years ago have already made a big difference to their community. Those children who slept in your spare bed, who ate your food, who you nursed through sickness, who you counseled through tears while we stayed in your homes. I promise you, those are the leaders of tomorrow's Africa.

Chapter 18

REPORT ON BETHANY VILLAGE

By Adam Ansel

In the Mukono District of Uganda near the small village of Nabitaka lies Bethany Village. Forty acres of land on the shore of Lake Victoria which currently holds a campsite, living area, a primary school, and are an active area of work showing the hand of God.

The first time I visited Bethany Village in early 2004 there were a scattering of buildings standing up among piles of building materials and overgrown grass, a beginning. In the year and a half that has passed since then, a complete shift has taken place. Gone are the piles of materials and gone is the tall grass and in place is a small piece of hope for the children of Uganda.

When you pull up to the dock jutting out into the lake and you first step ashore the first thing you see is the campsite. The campsite area is constantly being developed and improved upon with new buildings, walkways, and better facilities being installed weekly. Work is being done there to install drainage ditches so that rainwater properly flows to the lake instead of making gullets in the path. Recently new sleeping quarters were built for pastors and other guests to Bethany Village to use throughout their stays there.

They have a sleeping room and a bathroom with a shower and toilet.

The camping area is well developed now and camps are being run throughout the year with many children, youth, and adults staying there. The dorm rooms are capable of holding many guests and there are plenty of showers and toilets available. A pavilion has been built for gatherings and services, and there is a canteen for the supervisors to relax at after a hard days work.

Continuing on up the hill you come to the "home" area. Bethany Village is a refuge area for many different types of children who need to experience both the love of God and the love of a family. The real vision of this area of Bethany is to create a real African community with parents raising children in a loving, Christian environment. The children that make up this area are comprised of children from the village of Gaba as well as the villages surrounding Bethany. Some of them were street children, with no homes or families, living off the food they could find in the streets, others have been abused by family members and then chased away to survive on their own. Many of the children are true orphans with no fathers of mothers to take care of them, while others come from single parent homes where they can't be properly taken care of.

Currently Bethany Village has four active orphanage homes with fifteen to seventeen children staying in each one. Three of the homes have wonderful single ladies living there taking care of the children and being the mother that they have never had, while the fourth has a married couple living there giving the children a father figure as well. These mommies and daddies are sacrificing of themselves and living there, working full time to take care of these children with no electricity, far removed from the rest of the ministry in Gaba. They are a true blessing from God: they love the children so much.

Four more homes are nearing completion and will soon have children living in them. More are in the process of being built so soon many more children will be being raised in a loving, godly environment.

During the days the children are at school but in the evenings and on the weekends while they are home, the house parents work with them around the home and in the garden areas. They teach the children cooking skills and other basic things that show the children how to be self-sufficient.

An area of three and a half acres has been set aside for growing crops which are being sold to people in the surrounding areas as a way of making an income for the homes and each home has its own garden area growing a variety of fruits and vegetables for the children and adults living there.

There are many difficulties entailed with living in Bethany Village but one of the biggest is water. Each home is equipped with a very big water tank which collects rain water. Unfortunately during certain parts of the year rainfall is very infrequent and the tanks run dry quickly. There is a large water source nearby, Lake Victoria, but there are a number of problems with the lake. First of all, the lake is dirty, and this water is used for bathing, washing clothes, and drinking. Secondly, the children have to carry jerry cans down the hill to the lake and then all the way back up to the house, which is not an extremely long walk, but is uphill and many of the children are still young.

They tried to dig a community well and a lot of money was put into this project but unfortunately no water was discovered so they still have to rely on the lake and the rain to get their water. There are plans to install a hand pump for drawing water out of the ground but currently nothing is being done about it.

Earlier this year a fence was put up surrounding the entire plot of land that is Bethany Village. It skirts around the outer edge of the property, through the gardens, along the road and up the hill through the jungle. It's one way of keeping things organized and knowing where our boundaries are. The roads are still lopsided and full of holes due to runoff from the rainy season but other roads are being cleared and things are coming together very well.

When you reach the top of the hill, you have reached the school area of Bethany Village. The school currently has somewhere around four hundred children from baby class [pre-school] up to Primary Five [about fifth grade]. The nursery block has been finished and is now a permanent structure where the children can learn without having the rain fall on their heads or the wind blow their papers around while they try to study. The other Primary students are currently in a temporary wooden structure with no doors or windows and a dirt floor but the new permanent block has been started and within a few weeks the children will move into their new building as well. A hydroform machine has been brought over and workers are busy mixing sand, concrete, and soil together, then they put it into the machine and within a few seconds a brick comes out. They are capable of producing large quantities of bricks each day and these are being used in the construction of the children's homes as well as the primary school.

A clinic has been started up but as of right now it is functioning without a home. The project manager is using his home as a base for the clinic but this brings patients at all times of the day and night. After a hard day's work, he sometimes comes home to relax and has a line of people at the door waiting for treatment.

The nurse is busy dealing with many different cases, but mostly malaria. She is without a microscope though and most times she has to use her own professional judgment to determine the illness of the patient. There is no way for her to properly check the blood for the malaria without a microscope so that is a desperate need right now. Another problem is that most of the drugs needed for the various sicknesses are only available back in Gaba. The nurse has to take a boat across the lake and go to the new Wentz Medical Center in Gaba to fetch the drugs and then has to take them all the way back across the lake to hand them out.

Any serious illnesses or cases involving surgeries are referred to Wentz Medical Center but once again the patient must cross the lake to even get to the hospital.

As you stand on top of the hill and survey all of Bethany Village from the campsite down on the lakes edge, up past the children's homes, and around you at the Primary school you can truly see God's hand at work. Changes and improvements are being made at a rapid pace. There are still many challenges and a long road ahead until it becomes everything we dream of, but God is paving the way and the work that He has started, He will be faithful to complete. Many thanks to all of you for your prayers and support of Bethany Village. People of all ages are being helped from this project – from the elderly man who needs medicine to the small child who has been abandoned. Bethany Village has become a beacon of love and a tangible place where people can walk into the loving arms of people who love them back and will take care of them all in the name of our Lord Jesus Christ.

CONCLUSION

God has done and continues to do incredible things with Mwangaza. They continue to minister in their own community and are preparing for their next tour (in January 2006).

As I said in the preface, all I can tell you is my own story. I hope and pray that by reading the story of my tour that you have been given an insight into what we do and maybe a little bit of why we do it.

When I left tour, all of the children made me cards to say goodbye. Inside a card, one of the children had written, "Thanks for standing in Mom and Dad's gap." Of everything that happened during the tour, through the good times and the bad, that one phrase sticks in my mind as the reason I chose to do something so ill advised in the eyes of the world. I'm a reasonably good sound engineer and I can drive a van – that was my job on tour. It wasn't my reason for being there. The reason I was there was to stand in the gap for these children.

I'm 26 now – my own parents are (and have been for a few years) muttering about me settling down, finding a wife, getting a good job and that kind of thing. I tell people that I intend to work as a missionary in Africa and get a mixture of rolled eyes and looks of concern. It's lucky that we don't need to worry about what the world thinks – if I don't stand in 'mom and dad's gap,' then who will?

Every day, I wake up and ask God, 'Can I go to Africa yet?' Every day, God says, 'not just yet.' It's hard to know if you're in the will of God but I remain confident that I am where God wants me right now and that leaving tour was the right thing to do. God has other plans for my life – to mould and shape me in other directions. I pray that one day, I'll wake up and God will say 'Today is the day.'

Let me finish with something revolutionary. I believe that to a certain extent, God doesn't really care if I'm in Ireland, Uganda, America or Outer Mongolia. What he calls me to is a personal relationship with himself. Wherever I am in the world, I can do that. I can go to Africa if I choose. I can go back to Ireland if I choose. I can go to Siberia if I choose but I can still live a life within God's will in a relationship with Him. Circumstances in my life dictate that now is not the right time for me to go – I have debts to pay, projects to finish and maybe a few things still to learn before I am ready to move to Africa permanently.

But that's my story. What is your's? Don't wait around forever for God's call to go to Africa because chances are it won't come. Take a risk. Don't regret the things that you never did in your life. Sign up for a short term mission trip. Go to Gaba. See what you can do to help. Do it. According to WHO statistics, somewhere in the region of 6 million people will have died from hunger in the length of time it has taken to write this book. So once again, I say...

That's my story. What is your's? Don't wait around forever for God's call to go to Africa. Take a risk. Don't regret the things that you never did in your life. Sign up for a short term mission trip. Go to Gaba. See what you can do to help. Do it. It's that easy. Our house is just around the corner from the church. It's called Ennyumba ye Kitangaala (House of Light). And since you opened your house to me, let me return the favor – you take my bed, I'll sleep on the sofa.

MORE INFORMATION: HOW CAN I GET INVOLVED?

If you have read this book and feel that you want to get involved, there are a hundred and one things you could do. Going to Africa is one of them but is by no means the only way you can help. Africa Renewal Ministries is a growing organization and needs volunteers like you.

One way you could help is to join the touring staff – we need drivers, AV technicians, teachers, administrators, product managers, nurses but most importantly people who are available and willing to stand in the gap for these children. When I started, I 'knew nothing' about being a sound engineer as Craig so elegantly put it. But I learned and you can too. The important thing is that I was willing to be there for these children.

There are an army of people who work behind the scenes for Mwangaza – booking concerts, arranging host families and taking care of the day to day administration that keeps us on the road. They are all volunteers and we always need fresh input and new ideas in this work.

Africa Renewal Ministries has its own staff that takes care of the organization as a whole: administering the sponsorship, accountants, and business managers.

What we love are people with a vision. So many people feel that they need to start their own organization to do their own thing. If we work together, we can achieve greater things. If you have an idea or a vision or a dream or a plan, talk to us. We would love to work with you. We don't discriminate because of age, race or color. Some of the biggest assets to our organization are over 70 and under 20 years old.

One last word. If you don't agree with the way we go about our work or you have a problem with our staff, then I'm sorry. But please, don't let that put you off helping these children. If you don't help them through us, help them through another organization or agency. There are literally hundreds of great organizations doing what they can in Africa and around the world.

At the end of a Saturday night concert, a pastor once said, "I don't care if you come to our church tomorrow morning but please, at least go to a church – any church." My message is similar. I don't care if you don't support our organization but I beg you, please help these kids somehow. Anyhow. Because if you don't, who else will?

But even more important than that: regardless of whether you have enjoyed this book, could care less about Africa or have never even heard of Mwangaza, I don't care if you come to my church on Sunday morning but please, at least go to a church, any church. God is literally crying God-sized tears for every soul that he doesn't know.

Africa Renewal Ministries, Inc. is the US-based organization supporting Africa Renewal Ministries and is a registered 501(c)(3) corporation.

For Africa Renewal Ministries(USA) (the parent organization)
http://www.africarenewal.org
info@africarenewal.org

For Mwangaza Children's Choir
http://www.mwangazachoir.org
info@mwangazachoir.org

For mail or telephone enquiries for Mwangaza or ARM please contact

P.O. Box 781671
San Antonio, TX, 78278
Tel: (210) 979-7441

If you would like more copies of this book, please visit
   http://www.mwangazachoir.org

For information on the ongoing ministry of Mark McKnight and Adam Ansel, or more titles (including CDs and DVDs) by either please visit
   http://www.babymosquito.com
   http://www.ahymnforafrica.com

Or to contact directly, email to
   mark@mwangazchoir.org
   adam@mwangazachoir.org

All proceeds from this book will go directly towards the ministry of Africa Renewal Ministries in Africa and the Mwangaza Children's Choir on tour around the world.

On The Road
Mark McKnight & Adam Ansel

Cover Design © 2006 Mark Rhodes

1. Sarah Zawedde
2. Angella Magoba
3. James Teira
4. Lillian Teira
5. Joe David Cubillos
6. Joshua Kasawuli
7. Jackie Nakinda
8. Daphine Nassuna
9. Kara Klemcke
10. Priscilla Mirembe
11. Angella Nakato
12. William Kigozi
13. Malachi Kabaale
14. Joy Meeme
15. Leah Kisakye
16. Omega Naava
17. Tana Klemcke
18. Nicolas Bunjo
19. Corey Klemcke
20. Freedom Kitengejja
21. Marci Klemcke
22. Cissy Namaale
23. Ponsiano Mugaga
24. Martin Muyanja
25. Dorothy Nanteza
26. Gladys Nakivumbi
27. Mark McKnight
28. Dorothy Alinda
29. Jesca Naava
30. Adam Ansel
31. Dwayne Mugenyi
32. Dave Yingling